ALABAMA
MUSICIANS

ALABAMA MUSICIANS

MUSICAL HERITAGE *from the* HEART OF DIXIE

C.S. FUQUA

THE
History
PRESS

Published by The History Press
Charleston, SC 29403
www.historypress.net

Cover design by Natasha Momberger

First published 2011

ISBN 978.1.540229687

Library of Congress Cataloging-in-Publication Data
Fuqua, Christopher S., 1956-
Alabama musicians : musical heritage from the heart of Dixie / C.S. Fuqua.
p. cm.
Includes bibliographical references.

1. Musicians--Alabama--Biography. I. Title.
ML385.F92 2-11
780.92'2761--dc23
[B]
2011027331

To Bonnie, Tegan, Yukio and Hideko; Janet and David; Rick, Michie,
Kanako, Dick, Tonya, Beth and John; the Neo Epoque members;
and all who love music.

Contents

CONTENTS

About This Book

Alabama's contributions to music are broad and profound, from defining musical styles such as boogie-woogie and blues to providing major artists in every music genre and to developing and housing production studios that have become legendary. This book's first section provides a brief history of the state's musical regions and their contributions to music since the 1800s. The second section explores the lives of some of the major artists from the state.

Due to the vast accomplishments of Alabamians, readers may expect to find certain artists' biographies included here only to discover that they're not. The basic criterion for inclusion is that the artist, or at least a member of any included band, be a native Alabamian. Performers like Mississippi native Jimmy Buffett, Jamaica-born Eddie Kirkland, Florida native Bobby Goldsboro and Los Angeles native Debbie Bond are not included, even though they're regularly associated with Alabama. If any nonnative artist deserves inclusion, it's Debbie for her relentless promotion of Alabama music and musicians through the Alabama Blues Project's educational programs, concerts and CD releases. These artists would have been included, but due to project limitations, not even all Alabama native artists could be included. So don't stop your research of Alabama's musical contributions here. Visit the Alabama Blues Project, Alabama Jazz Hall of Fame and Alabama Music Hall of Fame websites for more complete lists of Alabama artists, including transplants, to help you on the way.

Much gratitude goes to the artists, photographers and organizations who have contributed directly to this project, including photo editor Peggy

Collins and the Alabama Tourism Department, Alabama Blues Project, Birmingham Public Library, Alabama Music Hall of Fame, Alabama Jazz Hall of Fame and photographer Carol M. Highsmith for images from her Library of Congress *America* collection. I also thank The History Press and editors Will McKay and Hilary McCullough for initiating and supporting this project.

Alabama's Contributions to Music

Early History

Documenting Alabama's contributions to the world of music would have been delayed by decades had it not been for the efforts of a few individuals determined in the early to mid-1900s to preserve the state's rich cultural heritage. One of those researchers was Ruby Pickens Tartt, who passionately collected Alabama slave stories, folklore and folk music, eventually becoming a valuable resource to the Library of Congress and guaranteeing that the state's early musical achievements would not be lost to time.

Born in 1880 in Livingston, Tartt relished local African American culture, especially its robust music and storytelling. After graduating Alabama State Normal College, Tartt studied under William Merritt Chase at Chase School of Art in New York but returned to Alabama to marry William Pratt Tartt in 1904 and to work in the Tartt family's bank. She later formed a friendship with New York native Carl Carmer, who taught at the University of Alabama (UA). She regaled him with numerous tales of rural folk life and music that he later used as the basis for his novel, *Stars Fell on Alabama*, styling one of the book's main characters on Tartt. But it wasn't until the Great Depression destroyed much of the Tartts' wealth that Ruby began her work to preserve the rich musical culture she so loved.

Taking a job with the Works Progress Administration, a New Deal agency designed to put millions of Americans back to work, Tartt chaired

Ruby Pickens Tartt.
*Courtesy of the Library
of Congress, Prints &
Photographs Division,
Lomax Collection.*

the local Federal Writers' Project that ran from 1936 to 1940, documenting life stories, folktales and folksongs of former slaves. This research garnered the attention of John A. Lomax, a Library of Congress ethnomusicologist. Although Newman I. White, an Alabama Polytechnic Institute instructor, had published in 1928 a collection of songs by Alabama African Americans, entitled *American Negro Folk-Songs*, most of the songs had come to him secondhand from white students who had learned them from African American acquaintances. It wasn't until Lomax solicited Tartt's assistance that Alabama's authentic musical culture gained national recognition.

Tartt spent four years assisting Lomax in and around Sumter County, recording the voices and songs of convicts, schoolchildren and everyday folk, including Dock Reed and Vera Hall Ward, now considered two of the twentieth century's greatest folk vocalists. Listeners around the world were introduced to those singers and Alabama music through Lomax's ten-volume record set, *The Ballad Hunter*, and the British Broadcasting Corporation series of American folksong releases during the 1950s that included Tartt's transcriptions of lyrics for the Sumter County songs. Lomax and his son Alan later featured other material recorded with Tartt's help in the releases *Afro-American Spirituals, Work Songs, and Ballads* and *Afro-American Blues and Game Songs.*

In the 1940s, Tartt contracted with Houghton Mifflin to base a collection of short stories on local culture, but a tornado struck her home, destroying her research and severely injuring her right hand. Although she never completed the book, she assisted folklorist Harold Courlander in 1950 to record more Sumter County singers, who were included in the Folkways collections *Rich Amerson I, Rich Amerson II, Folk Music U.S.A., Negro Folk Music of Alabama, Negro Songs of Alabama* and *Negro Folk Music U.S.A.* Many of the songs appeared in subsequent collections and were covered by artists such as the Kingston Trio. Since Tartt's death on November 29, 1974, new audiences have been introduced to early Alabama folk life through the songs, stories and lore that she collected.

In 1938, Byron Arnold, an Eastman School of Music of New York graduate, joined UA's music department and became enamored with African American preaching and singing and the music's cultural importance. While

Alabama singer Uncle Rich Brown (right) and John A. Lomax near Sumterville. *Courtesy of the Library of Congress, Prints & Photographs Division, Lomax Collection.*

Tartt and Lomax concentrated efforts in and around Sumter County, Arnold explored music by black and white residents statewide. Then, in 1945, with UA Research Committee financial support, Arnold enlisted Tartt's help and spent that summer touring the state to transcribe tunes and lyrics to paper. Even though he had no recording device, Arnold viewed the trip as a success, transcribing 258 folksongs.

In 1946, Arnold borrowed a device to record Gallic Craven, one of the best singers he'd heard, making three double-faced recordings before she died that summer. Following her death, he continued to explore rural area music, expanding his transcriptions by another 226. The following year, UA provided additional funds for a recording device, but it failed to arrive by summer. So Arnold set out with another borrowed device, making 100 ten-inch recordings, delighted that the singers performed "quietly, naturally, never dramatically, and entirely without the mannerisms and clichés of the concert soloist." During the 1947–48 academic year, copyrights on two songs he'd recorded earned ten dollars for the university—the only project, the Research Committee secretary noted, that had ever made money. In 1950, the UA Press published *Folksongs of Alabama*, containing 153 of the collected songs.

Even as folksong societies sprang up and Arnold became a popular lecturer around the state, he decided to take a job at California State University in Los Angeles, where he began work on his doctorate in classical music at the University of Southern California. His research and work on Alabama music thus ended, and he never returned to it. Arnold died in 1971, leaving his folksong material to UA, which published many of the songs in the 2004 release *An Alabama Songbook: Ballads, Folksongs, and Spirituals.*

THAT JAZZ AND MORE

Alabama's folk artists and culture gained worldwide recognition in the early and mid-1900s because of efforts by Tartt, Lomax, Arnold and other folksong researchers. But even as the world recognized the state's folk contributions, Alabama was profoundly affecting other music genres as well.

Thanks to 1800s Scots-Irish and African influences—from Birmingham's steel mills to Mobile's coastal life—fiddles and banjos spiced up the sound of Alabama's folk music during the late 1800s and early 1900s, spawning popular string bands that encompassed guitars, spoons and washboards

Shape notes.

and elevated the fiddle to a primary instrument as the music evolved into bluegrass. On another front, African American vocal traditions became part of more sophisticated styles such as the blues. Both blues and bluegrass/country bands have influenced an array of Alabama artists, from W.C. Handy and Hank Williams Sr. to the Louvin Brothers and many others who've combined genres into new styles to appeal to ever-broadening audiences.

Gospel, too, played an important role in Alabama music, especially the style known as Sacred Harp singing, or shape-note singing, sung from tune books that utilize note symbols that help singers define pitch within major and minor scales without the traditional information in the staff's key signatures. Brothers Seaborn and Thomas Denson, who grew up on a farm in Cleburne County in the mid-1800s, performed and wrote shape-note songs for a half century while conducting singing schools across the South. Thomas's son Paine revised and published their original book of Sacred Harp songs after their deaths in the mid-1930s, entitling it *Original Sacred Harp (Denson Revision): The Best Collection of Sacred Songs, Hymns, Odes and Anthems Ever Offered the Singing Public for General Use.* The 1991 revision is commonly referred to as the Denson book.

Throughout the early 1900s, styles merged and evolved, providing platforms for some of the most notable artists in history. But despite the level of emerging talent, state venues remained racially segregated, an accepted practice since the 1819 document that created Alabama. Even after the Civil War in 1868, when African Americans were legally enfranchised, the 1875 Alabama Constitution constrained black political power through gerrymandering, political appointments, restrictive voter registration dates and requirements and ballots listing candidates but not party affiliation. Then, the 1901 constitutional convention effectively established a state based on white supremacy and class division, eliminating home rule for counties and centralizing power in the capital, setting limits on property taxes, creating a regressive tax system that continues to burden those least able to afford it, restricting voting rights to disenfranchise both blacks and working-class whites, establishing a segregated school system and enabling subsequent legislatures to further the segregationist agenda.

Segregation governed every aspect of life, even entertainment, resulting in a venue network that catered specifically to African American audiences from the 1800s through the 1960s. To serve these segregated establishments, promoters and black venue owners across the country formed the Theater Owners Booking Association (TOBA), quickly dubbed by musicians and performers as "Tough on Black Asses" due to substandard pay and conditions. The circuit ran from Chicago to New York, Baltimore, the South, the Midwest and the West Coast. In the 1930s, business fell off considerably due to the nation's economic downturn. The Great Depression forced some venues along the circuit to close completely, while others moved into homes, barns, apartments and old shacks. The circuit soon became known as the Chitlin' Circuit because chitterlings (boiled or fried pig intestines) and other southern soul foods were served in many of the establishments.

Although performers such as Duke Ellington, Billie Holiday and Count Basie appealed to both black and white audiences, segregation laws restricted artists to Chitlin' Circuit venues. One of the most famous collections of venues was in Birmingham's Fourth Avenue District. Black

Birmingham's Colored Masonic Temple. *Photo by C.S. Fuqua.*

and white businesses had developed side by side in most downtown areas before 1890, but Jim Crow laws eliminated the practice, and the Fourth Avenue District became a black business district—black-owned for a black clientele. The district also served as a social and cultural center for African Americans, mirroring activities in predominantly white districts. Businesses ran the gamut from beauty shops to mortuaries, from saloons and theaters to motels, but it's the Fourth Avenue District's nightlife for which the area's remembered. The level of entertainment made it *the* place to be, especially for jazz. Monroe Kennedy, a blind booking agent, brought in the day's best swing bands, many performing in the seven-story Colored Masonic Temple, a favorite of performers such as Duke Ellington and Louis Armstrong. It was Birmingham native Erskine Hawkins, however, who secured the district's place in jazz history.

The area near a streetcar crossing on the Ensley-Fairfield line buzzed with nightlife activity, thanks to a glut of juke joints and ballrooms. Mill and

Graduating hundreds of professional musicians from Birmingham Industrial High School, John T. "Fess" Whatley became one of the most influential educators in American music. *Courtesy of the Alabama Music Hall of Fame.*

railroad workers wanted to look their best when they went out, so many rented tuxedos, and the area soon became known as Tuxedo Junction. One of the most popular Tuxedo Junction spots was a dance hall on the second floor of the Nixon-Belcher Building. Hawkins—a graduate of Birmingham Industrial High School, where he learned music under the instruction of John T. "Fess" Whatley—formed a band with other schoolmates, including Haywood Henry and Bob Range. Inspired by the music he'd heard while growing up in the district, Hawkins wrote the instrumental "Tuxedo Junction." The publishing company sent the song to lyricist Buddy Feyne, who, after consulting with Hawkins, penned lyrics that will forever tie the song to Birmingham's Fourth Avenue District. The Erskine Hawkins Orchestra's original version rose to number seven on the national hit parade, while the Glenn Miller Orchestra took it to *Billboard*'s number one position in 1939.

By the end of the 1960s, the Chitlin' Circuit had ironically succumbed to the positive results of the civil rights movement. Racial barriers had begun to crumble, and the Fourth Avenue District fell into disrepair as patrons left for other venues, forcing business owners to shutter their establishments. During the 1990s, however, the city revitalized the district, and today it's again home to several African American–owned businesses and the Birmingham Civil Rights Institute. The Carver Theater, which offered first-run movies to the district's black audiences when it was built in 1934, is now home to the

Birmingham's Carver Theater, now housing the Alabama Jazz Hall of Fame. *Courtesy of the Alabama Jazz Hall of Fame.*

Alabama Jazz Hall of Fame, honoring Alabama's jazz greats and related professionals such as disc jockeys and music journalists who influenced Alabama's jazz heritage.

Even as crumbling barriers between the races brought an end to the Chitlin' Circuit and its once thriving venues in Birmingham and other cities, new freedom led to extraordinary opportunities for both black and white artists from the late 1950s through the 1970s. Those new opportunities would eventually transform a four-town area in Alabama's northwest corner into the Hit Recording Capital of the World.

THE 1960S AND BEYOND

As social changes effectively shut down the Chitlin' Circuit and the Fourth Avenue District, new opportunities developed, leading a few musical mavericks from Alabama to open recording studios that would become legendary. Flowing one into another, Florence, Sheffield, Tuscumbia and Muscle Shoals are collectively known as the Shoals. With metals, chemicals, rubber products and agriculture the primary industries, the

W.C. Handy home, Florence. *Photo by Tegan Fuqua.*

Shoals is the birthplace and childhood home of Helen Keller, W.C. Handy and Sam Phillips.

The area's transformation into a recording center began in the 1930s, when Dexter and Ray Johnson's family moved from Mississippi to the Shoals. Over the next three years, the boys established themselves in the local music scene and became a familiar feature on local radio. At age seventeen, Dexter left, lured to Detroit for fifteen-dollar-a-night gigs instead of the four-dollar gigs available in Mississippi and Alabama. But three years proved enough, and Dexter returned to the Shoals, married and took a job as an assistant turbine operator at the Tennessee Valley Authority's steam-powered electric generating plant. In 1942, he and brother Ray joined with Quinton Claunch, Buddy Bain and Bill Cantrell to form the country band the Blue Seal Pals, with Dexter on upright bass. The group became a regular on WJOI in Florence and later on WSM in Nashville, hosting the Saturday morning program *Sunup Serenade*. When the band began to tour,

Dexter Johnson and the Blue Seal Pals. *Courtesy of the Alabama Music Hall of Fame.*

Dexter resigned his day job to play, while Ray chose to leave the band. The band toured the next seven years with headline performers such as Cowboy Copas, but in 1949, weary of the road, the Pals disbanded, and Dexter returned to his old job with TVA.

Unable to shake his desire to make music, Dexter converted his garage into a basic recording studio, unwittingly setting the area on a new path. Dexter equipped his studio with a monaural tape recorder and began engineering radio programs and demos for as-yet-unknown performers such as Melba Montgomery and thirteen-year-old Tanya Tucker. Although he had no hit records of his own during his career, Dexter played as a studio musician on the 1957 hit "White Silver Sands" by Dave Gardner, recorded in Memphis. In the 1980s, West Germany's Cattle Records issued several albums of Dexter's performances.

While Dexter provided basic recording services to area musicians, it was Shoals native James Joiner who brought notoriety to the area in the 1950s.

Buddy Killen. *Courtesy of the Alabama Music Hall of Fame.*

Joiner, who died in 2007, wrote the song "A Fallen Star" after witnessing a late-night meteor streak across the sky. He recruited high school student Bobby Denton for vocals and recorded the song during a four-dollar session at local WLAY radio studio. Joiner recruited former army buddy and guitarist Kelton "Kelso" Herston, Walter Stovall and Marvin Wilson to form Tune Records in 1956 to release the single, while Buddy Killen, another Shoals native, published the song through his Nashville-based Tree Music company. Originally a bass player, Killen had become a prominent music publisher and record producer in Nashville, later working with artists such as Dolly Parton, Rascal Flatts and Reba McEntire. The song became a regional hit for Denton, but cover versions by Jimmy C. Newman and Ferlin Husky made the song a national hit.

Herston soon moved to Nashville, and Denton left music to start a family and later entered politics. Meanwhile, Joiner and Tom Stafford formed Spar Music in 1959, but Joiner later sold his shares to Stafford to concentrate fully on Tune, following "A Fallen Star" with another of his songs, "Lovely Work of Art," in 1960, performed by Jimmy C. Newman. By then, aspiring Alabama songwriters and musicians had begun to migrate to the Shoals as word of Tune's initial success spread. Billy Sherrill and Rick Hall, both from Phil Campbell and members of the Fairlanes band, made weekly trips to the Shoals to pitch songs to Joiner, who published several, including "Aching, Breaking Heart" and "Sweet and Innocent."

Born in 1932, about forty miles from Muscle Shoals in Freedom Hills, Hall received his introduction to music from his father, a sawmill worker who loved southern gospel music and provided ten-day singing lessons for extra money. In 1944, the Hall family moved to Cleveland, Ohio, where Hall's father worked in a defense plant until the end of the war, when the family moved back to Alabama to sharecrop. Having developed a liking for country music, Hall attended a rural school and joined a Future Farmers of America string band that won first and second places in successive years in statewide competition. Hall dropped out of school in his junior year, moving to Rockford, Illinois, in 1951 to play nights in a band for tips and beer and work days as a tool-and-die apprentice. Drafted in 1952, Hall entered the army as a conscientious objector. On leave before scheduled deployment to Korea as a medic, Hall wrecked his car after a night out drinking, breaking his back and requiring a year of rehabilitation. By the time he returned to duty, the war was over, and Hall joined the Fourth Army Honor Guard, playing in a band that featured Faron Young and Gordon Terry.

Rick Hall and the Fairlanes. *Courtesy of the Alabama Music Hall of Fame.*

Following military service, Hall returned to Alabama and married in 1955, taking a job with Reynolds Aluminum in Florence but continuing to play music as a hobby. Eighteen months after his wedding, his wife died in a car crash. Two weeks later, his father died in a tractor accident. Hall quit his job and began to drink excessively, but he stuck with music, playing regularly in the Country Pals band throughout north Alabama, where he met and formed a friendship with Billy Sherrill of the Rhythm Swingers. The two began collaborating on songs and eventually formed the R&B-oriented Fairlanes.

After selling his shares to Stafford, Joiner introduced Stafford to Hall and Sherrill, and Stafford offered them a partnership, suggesting they should write, publish and market their own work. The three converted space above Florence City Drugstore into a primitive recording studio, soundproofing one small room's walls with egg cartons and heavy window drapes, dividing it from a second room by a window in the common wall. A tiny table in the second room supported a Berlant-Concertone tape recorder. With the addition of three microphones and a mixer, the Florence Alabama Music Enterprises recording studio, better known as FAME, opened for business, blessed with changing social attitudes that had led to the Chitlin' Circuit's demise. Joiner, meanwhile, despite Tune's moderate success, decided to return to the family bus business.

As FAME went forward, stress eventually drove a wedge in the relationship among Hall, Sherrill and Stafford. Hall pressed the others for increasingly more studio production even as the company produced demos for local musicians and signed numerous local writers, including Dan Penn and Arthur Alexander. In 1960, the original FAME dissolved, with Sherrill and Stafford retaining the record label and Hall taking the publishing company and the name FAME, moving his operation to a low-rent warehouse. Although musicians and writers continued to work at the business above the drugstore, once again called Spar Music, the company never released another record. Sherrill eventually went to work for area native Sam Phillips, who had opened Sun Records in Memphis. Meanwhile, Hall's determination to succeed with FAME led him to the funky sound of R&B, which had been growing in popularity among black and white audiences alike.

To finance the business, Hall took a job at the used car lot of his future father-in-law, Hansel Cross, who became a silent partner to help Hall secure a loan to purchase basic recording equipment. While living in the studio at first, Hall utilized various everyday materials such as burlap to create desired recording sound effects. And even though he and Sherrill were no longer partners, they continued to play together in the Fairlanes on weekends as Hall worked weekdays selling cars and weeknights recording local musicians such as Jerry Carrigan and David Briggs.

Arthur Alexander's "You Better Move On" became FAME's first hit. Using Peanut Montgomery, Terry Thompson, Carrigan and Briggs for the session, Hall used three microphones to record the song, with only one devoted to both Montgomery's guitar and Alexander's vocals. Unable to interest any Nashville record company in the song, Hall pitched it to California-based Dot Records, which picked it up. The song reached number twenty-four on *Billboard*'s Hot 100 and was later recorded by the Rolling Stones.

In 1962, the owner of the warehouse housing FAME nearly tripled rent, and Hall decided to build his own studio, securing another loan with the help of his father-in-law and a first cousin who was a vice-president at First Federal Savings and Loan in Florence. That loan built a studio that measured twenty feet by seventy feet with an eighteen-foot ceiling. Another loan from a Tuscumbia bank furnished it with recording equipment. As royalties on

The original FAME Studio. *Courtesy of the Alabama Music Hall of Fame.*

Alexander's song helped pay off the loans, Hall paid operational bills by renting studio time to local musicians, including a band called the Del Rays. The group's guitarist, Jimmy Johnson, impressed Hall enough to become FAME's first employee, filling various roles, including janitor, musician, engineer and bookkeeper.

FAME's moderate success drew the attention of Bill Lowery, who provided acts to ABC, including those he decided to bring to FAME such as Tommy Roe, the Tams and Mac Davis. Hall's recordings of Roe's "Everybody" and the Tams' "What Kind of Fool" became hits and ensured further work with Lowery. At the same time, R&B acts actively sought out FAME for recording, and Hall found himself at the forefront of social change by working with black artists, which proved extremely profitable.

After completing work with Lowery's initial artists, Hall next charted with "Steal Away," a song recorded but shelved before FAME's first hit, "You Better Move On." Believing in the song's potential with Jimmy Hughes on vocals, Hall modeled "Steal Away" after the 1959 hit "Candy Apple Red." Pressing the record himself rather than continuing to pitch it to producers, Hall traveled to black radio stations around the Southeast to secure airplay. The record proved wildly popular, but the recording plant Hall used demanded cash on delivery for records pressed—money Hall didn't have. Lowery, after working with Hall, stepped in as liaison with LA's Vee Jay Records, which picked up the record for distribution in 1964. "Steal Away" reached the Top 20, but Vee Jay went out of business due to legal fees incurred in battling for rights to the Beatles' music.

Soon after Vee Jay's collapse, the musicians who worked most of FAME's sessions decided to move to bigger markets, and Hall replaced them with novices, including Jimmy Johnson on guitar, Junior Lowe on bass, Roger Hawkins on drums and Spooner Oldham on keyboards. Working diligently over the next two years, the musicians developed a sound that would eventually distinguish the Shoals from other recording centers in the United States.

By 1966, Hall had begun turning away demo business to develop acts he thought promising. To capitalize on the demo market, Marlin Greene and Quin Ivy, who'd been writing songs with Hall, opened Quinvy Studio, a small recording studio that regularly borrowed FAME's studio musicians for sessions, paying them with studio time. Ivy's break came while visiting a friend hospitalized at the Colbert County Hospital, where he met Percy Sledge, who worked as an orderly and sang on weekends for the Esquires frat circuit band. Ivy invited Sledge to Quinvy Studio to record a song that would become "When a Man Loves a Woman" after Ivy's rewrite of the lyrics. Johnson engineered the final version, which Ivy took to Hall, who sent it to Jerry Wexler of Atlantic Records. Wexler bought the rights from Ivy for $1,000 and 8 percent royalties. Of that 8 percent, 1 percent went to Hall as a finder's fee (along with another percent from Wexler), 3 percent to Sledge, 2 to Greene as co-producer and 2 to Ivy. Wexler and Ivy split publishing profits fifty-fifty. Hall, who had rights to the record's B side, did well monetarily, but more importantly, the song brought Atlantic Records to FAME. Seven weeks after its debut at one hundred in February 1966, the song went to number one, Atlantic's third top hit.

Another hit like "When a Man Loves a Woman" never materialized for Ivy, and in 1973, he decided to pursue other interests. For Hall and Johnson, the song established a professional relationship with Wexler, who'd been using Stax studios in Memphis but now brought his artists to FAME to establish the Shoals as a major R&B recording center with acts like Wilson Pickett, who cut his first Top 10 hit, "Land of a 1,000 Dances," at FAME. But both Wexler and Hall liked to be in charge, and friction soon sparked.

The first spark came when Wexler took Pickett there to record "Mustang Sally" and "Funky Broadway." Wexler didn't use all of FAME's personnel, instead bringing his own engineer, as well as replacing FAME's bassist, Junior Lowe, with Memphis bassist Tommy Cogbill. The second spark came in 1967, when Wexler took Aretha Franklin to FAME. The session for "I Never Loved a Man (the Way I Love You)" went flawlessly. But the second session for "Do Right Woman, Do Right Man" deteriorated as the afternoon progressed. Someone introduced whiskey into the mix, and tongues loosened with crude comments that led to flaring tempers. Hall abruptly fired one of the session horn musicians over a racist remark to Franklin, and the session ended in turmoil. Wexler blamed the fiasco on Hall for not having hired the session players he'd requested. Fearing he'd lose Wexler's business altogether, Hall went to Franklin's hotel to apologize for the fracas, but that meeting erupted into a physical confrontation between Hall and Franklin's husband, Ted White. By morning, Franklin and White had left for New York, followed that afternoon by Wexler, but not before he told Hall that their professional relationship was over. Even so, he asked Hall for the loan of the FAME rhythm section, telling him that he needed the musicians in New York for the album *King Curtis Plays the Memphis Hits*. What he planned, though, was to use the section to record the B side for "Do Right Woman, Do Right Man."

The Muscle Shoals rhythm section. *Left to right*: Roger Hawkins, Barry Beckett, Jimmy Johnson and David Hood. *Courtesy of the Alabama Music Hall of Fame.*

When Hall agreed, hoping the good-faith gesture would bring Wexler back to FAME, drummer Roger Hawkins, keyboardist Spooner Oldham and guitarist Jimmy Johnson left for New York. Hall later learned that Wexler had lied, and he became furious and immediately booked sessions at FAME to get the section back home, determined to limit their outside work from then on. By then, the rhythm section had earned great respect from the numerous acts recording at FAME and were known as musicians who could easily accommodate an array of talents and styles. When keyboardist Barry Beckett replaced Oldham, who left to work in Memphis, and bassist David Hood joined, the section became complete and developed a musical signature that became known as the "Muscle Shoals sound," what Hall described as "funky, hard, gutty, down to earth…warm and heartfelt with a dance beat."

As Hall demanded exclusivity from the section, Wexler and other outside producers continued to court the section for freelance work. Resulting tension between the section and Hall finally led to the section's decision to go into business for themselves. Delighted, Wexler provided funds for the section to purchase a one-time coffin warehouse on Jackson Highway in Sheffield for conversion into a small studio. The section paid Wexler back

The original Muscle Shoals Sound Studio. *Photo by Tegan Fuqua.*

in studio time. Over the years, Wexler eventually moved his R&B work to Miami. Although he tried to persuade the section to move as well, the group remained at home in the Shoals.

Meanwhile, Hall signed a significant contract with Capitol Records to produce artists on FAME's own record label. With the old section gone, Hall assembled a new group of musicians, including FAME veteran Junior Lowe on guitar, Jesse Boyce on bass, Freeman Brown on drums and Clayton Ivy on keyboards. He also assembled the Muscle Shoals Horns. In September 1969, *Newsweek* magazine asserted that Muscle Shoals was trying to be to R&B what Nashville was to country music, but nothing stays the same.

As a kid, Jimmy Johnson developed an interest in recording and hung around his Uncle Dexter Johnson's converted garage studio to learn all his uncle could teach him about record production. A self-taught guitarist, Johnson decided to pursue music as a profession upon graduation from high school. Through the years as a studio musician and band member, Johnson's goal became to open his own studio. When the opportunity arose for the rhythm section, Johnson was ready. With a defined, popular sound, section members considered several ideas for a studio name, and then Hood suggested the Muscle Shoals Sound—a "raw, funky sound on the very edge

The Alabama Music Hall of Fame. *Photo by Tegan Fuqua.*

of tightness and looseness," according to Johnson. The name provided immediate identity for the studio by capitalizing on the section's distinctive reputation. Later on, the rhythm section became known by another name as well when Leon Russell tagged them as the Swampers, and Lynyrd Skynyrd popularized them by that name in "Sweet Home Alabama."

Atlantic's first artist at Muscle Shoals Sound was Cher, who entitled her album with the studio's street address, *3614 Jackson Highway*, but the album didn't sell well, and it took nearly a year before the studio scored its first hit with R.B. Greaves's song "Take a Letter, Maria," followed by Greaves's "There's Always Something There to Remind Me." During the December 1969 Greaves sessions, the Rolling Stones, taking a short break from their tour, flew in to record with Johnson as engineer. In three days, the band cut three songs—"Wild Horses," "Brown Sugar" and "You Gotta Move"— starting sessions at 6:00 p.m. each day. Johnson played guitar for the daytime

Erskine Hawkins cuts the ribbon on the Alabama Music Hall of Fame's opening day, July 26, 1990. *Photo by C.S. Fuqua.*

Greaves sessions and engineered at night for the Stones. After rehearsing the first two hours each night, the Stones would complete the writing for the slated song and then begin recording in the third or fourth hour.

In following years, dozens of top artists recorded at the Sound, from Lulu and Herbie Mann to Joe Cocker, J.J. Cale, Boz Scaggs, Leon Russell, Bob Seger, Traffic, Paul Simon and many more, most completely satisfied with the results. Simon, for example, booked the studio for three days to cut one song, "Take Me to the Mardi Gras," but the rhythm section finished the song within two hours on the first day. Over the next two days, the section and Simon recorded "Kodachrome," "St. Judy's Comet" and "One Man's Ceiling, Another Man's Floor," all for the album *There Goes Rhymin' Simon*. The ability to learn and record a song quickly only added to the section's demand.

As the Shoals attracted more artists—pop and country at FAME, rock and folk at Muscle Shoals Sound—other studios opened, including Wishbone Recording Studio and Widget Studio, with all studio operators forming the Muscle Shoals Music Association (MSMA) to facilitate cooperation between the studios and to promote the Shoals recording industry. Hall told *Cash Box* in 1977, "It was dog eat dog. I was out to get them, and they were out to get me." The departure of musicians and engineers from FAME to other studios eventually necessitated cooperation to ensure survival through the borrowing and lending of talent from one another. In 1975, Hall served as the MSMA's first president. One of the MSMA's lasting achievements culminated in 1980 when the Alabama state legislature created the Alabama Music Hall of Fame Board, charged with developing a facility to honor Alabama music achievers. The resulting Alabama Music Hall of Fame (AMHoF) opened in Tuscumbia in July 1990.

During the late 1970s, Hall's pace slowed due to health-related issues, while Muscle Shoals Sound moved operations to a much larger thirty-one-thousand-square-foot building on the Tennessee River. Thanks to production quality, musicianship and writers such as George Johnson, who wrote "Old Time Rock & Roll," one of Bob Seger's most enduring hits, the Sound's notoriety grew internationally, and the studio hosted artists from around the world, including Japan, Sweden, Canada and France. But a downturn in the economy in 1980 caused the flow of artists to the Shoals to slow to a trickle, forcing smaller Shoals studios to close their doors. In 1985, Johnson and the section sold Muscle Shoals Sound to Mississippi-based Malaco. Hall, however, countered the economic downturn by taking FAME in yet another direction. Having established the company firmly with R&B and pop acts, Hall now concentrated on production of country acts, again showing his production prowess with Mac Davis's *Texas in My Rearview Mirror*, a hit album on both country and pop charts. His success drew other country acts that included Larry Gatlin, Gus Hardin, Terri Gibbs, Jerry Reed and T.G. Sheppard.

At the other end of the state, Mobile-based Integrity Media also proved that Alabama's recording industry could flourish in economically challenging times. Founded in 1987 by Sanford Kulkin and Mike Coleman as a direct-to-consumer music club called Integrity Music, the company evolved into Integrity Media, Inc., and expanded services to include production, publishing and distribution of Christian music and materials throughout the world, with offices in Tennessee, Singapore, South Africa and the United Kingdom. In 2002, the company purchased Nashville-based INO Records, which produced artists such as MercyMe, Sara Groves and the Afters, adding to Integrity's vast stable that already included Paul Baloche and Don Moen. Since that purchase, Integrity Music and INO have become two of the top independent labels of Christian music.

Barry Beckett, Bob Dylan and Jerry Wexler at Muscle Shoals Sound Studio. *Courtesy of the Alabama Music Hall of Fame.*

Back in the Shoals, FAME sold its publishing catalog to EMI in 1989, and Hall formed another company with sons Mark, Rodney and Rick Jr. The company's songwriters continued to write hit songs for various artists throughout the 1990s, including Pam Tillis, Reba McEntire and Shenandoa. In 1999, after FAME Publishing sold some of its catalogue to Music and Media, Hall's sons bought his remaining shares of stock, allowing him to concentrate on production. In 2001, the company established Muscle Shoals Records with an artist roster that includes Dylan LeBlanc, Jason Isbell, Gary Nichols, Angela Hacker and Jaime Fox.

Once a recording destination for artists ranging from Lynyrd Skynyrd to Willie Nelson and Bob Dylan, the second Muscle Shoals Sound studio was put up for sale in 2004 by owner Malaco, which originally bought the studio for its publishing catalogue with little interest in continuing recording services. In 2005, that studio closed for good. Meanwhile, the original Muscle Shoals Sound studio at 3614 Jackson Highway nearly vanished altogether. In the years following the section's move to the second Sound location, the building housed an appliance dealer and then a record store before being abandoned. In 1999, the city slated the rundown structure for demolition, but Noel Webster purchased, renovated and restored it to a recording facility, preserving aspects such as the bathroom door and portions of the bathroom wall and vocal booths that had been signed by such artists as Wilson Pickett and Cat Stevens. The restored Muscle Shoals Sound—equipped with replicas of the vintage recording equipment used in the original facility—is now listed on the National Register of Historic Places and is open to the public for tours and to musicians as a working recording studio.

Alabama has repeatedly proved itself a rich musical resource, with new stars rising each year. As the business of music adapts to an ever-changing world of technology and taste, one constant remains—the need for talent—and Alabama has and remains a state with a ready supply.

BIOGRAPHIES

Alabama

Forming a business alliance with relatives often proves disastrous. Not so with three cousins from Fort Payne who, along with the group's drummer from 1979 into the twenty-first century, proved to be one of the most successful acts in country music. Randy Owen and Jeff Cook, both born in 1949, and Teddy Gentry, born in 1952, formed the band Wild Country in 1977 while in college but changed the name to Alabama two years later when they added drummer and Massachusetts native Mark Herndon to spice up the group's country sound with a rock beat. One year later, their single "My Home's in Alabama" earned the group *Cashbox* magazine's New Vocal Group of the Year designation. Signing with RCA, Alabama went on to become one of the top country music acts of all time, garnering forty-two number one singles and winning more than 150 industry awards by the time the group officially disbanded. The full band played its last show in Bismarck, North Dakota, in October 2004.

Critics credit the band's success to tight vocal harmonies and lyrics that focus on working people such as "Forty-Hour Week," a song that pays tribute to steel mill and auto workers, farmers and food servers. With those assets, the band took risks others had not taken before, performing as a group rather than a single with a backing band and developing a powerful sound with special lighting to play large arenas and stadiums, venues more often used by rock bands. Despite the success and travels, the band's three cousins maintained their home base in the Fort Payne area. For several years, the group hosted the annual June Jam festival, with profits going to Fort Payne

Fort Payne's tribute to Alabama. *Photo by Karim Shamsi-Basha, courtesy of the Alabama Tourism Department.*

community charities and schools. A museum in Fort Payne now houses information and paraphernalia in tribute to the band.

Following the band's initial retirement, the cousins pursued individual projects until reuniting in 2006 to record the gospel *Songs of Inspiration* album, debuting at number one on *Billboard's* Top Country Albums, Top Christian/Gospel Albums and Top Current Contemporary Christian Albums, marking the first Alabama project to debut at number one on any chart. They followed with *Songs of Inspiration, Vol. II,* to capitalize further on the popularity of gospel albums by country artists.

In June 2008, Herndon joined with the cousins in Fort Payne for the unveiling of bronze statues to honor the group in Fort Payne City Park, but tension between Herndon and the others overshadowed festivities. After Herndon's earlier request for $65,047 as his share of the advance on the album *The Last Stand*, a live Alabama project being sold in Cracker Barrel stores, the cousins filed a lawsuit, claiming that Herndon had already been wrongly paid $202,670 for merchandise sales from the band's American Farewell Tour in 2003. In 2010, further legal problems arose for the cousins when Australian country music artist Allan Caswell, who wrote "On the Inside," the theme song for the Australian television show *Prisoner*, claimed that Alabama had used his song's melody for their song "Christmas in Dixie."

As fans long for a permanent band reunion, the cousins make random appearances together like the one in April 2011 at the Forty-sixth Annual Academy of Country Music Awards, joining Brad Paisley onstage to sing his song "Old Alabama." The former members have expressed no plans to reunite permanently, however, and continue to pursue individual projects.

Billy Bang

Born in Mobile on September 20, 1947, Billy Walker learned that you have to improvise life, just like jazz, to make it come out right. Walker's family moved to New York shortly after he was born, and he grew up in Harlem, listening to music from jazz clubs and businesses that blared artists like Eddie Harris and Dave Brubeck through street speakers during the 1950s. His first venture into performance was with bongos on the subway system as he and his friends took turns dancing and playing for extra money.

About the same time teachers selected Walker as a student who'd fit in well with his school's new music department, friends began calling him Billy Bang, purportedly after a cartoon character of the time, and the name stuck. Bang had wanted to play drums or sax, but teachers assigned him to violin, in part because he was too small for bass or cello. For two years, he studied classical music. Then, in ninth grade, a Massachusetts prep school offered him a hardship scholarship, and Bang accepted but quickly discovered he had little in common with the new school's students, who included Jackie Robinson Jr. and Arlo Guthrie. He left the school after two years to attend a high school in the Bronx but dropped out only to be drafted into the U.S. Army at age nineteen as fighting in Vietnam intensified.

Bang landed in Vietnam six months later and spent the next year as an infantry soldier. The fighting, politics and return home changed him completely, and he felt deep disappointment in himself and others and betrayed by his government. His homecoming proved even more disheartening when he found many of his friends addicted to drugs. Emotionally confused and floating, he

Billy Bang. *Photo by and courtesy of Stephen Johnson.*

joined what he called an "insurrectionist kind of group" similar to the Black Panthers, and he began gunrunning, transporting weapons to the group from southern states where purchase was easy. In a pawnshop to buy weapons on one run, he also bought a violin for twenty bucks, and his life changed.

He soon entered Queens College under the GI Bill as a pre-law student and began practicing violin in the park. His girlfriend suggested a move to the East Village, where other musicians gathered, and he began playing more seriously, finding that it soothed post-traumatic symptoms from his firefights in Vietnam. Eventually, he threw himself completely into improving his ability on violin. He soon earned a respectable reputation, developing a style that distinguished him from others in bands that performed "loft jazz," small avant-garde jazz concerts in New York lofts.

Bang formed the Survival Ensemble in the early 1970s and then cofounded the String Trio of New York in 1977 with bassist John Lindberg and guitarist

James Emery. In the mid-1980s, he moved briefly to the funk band Forbidden Planet and collaborated on projects with musicians who included pianist Marilyn Crispell and trumpeter Don Cherry. In 1992, he joined bassist John Ore, drummer Andrew Cyrille and pianist Sun Ra in what's believed to be Sun Ra's last recording session, producing the CD *Tribute to Stuff Smith*.

Perhaps his most remarkable work to date is *Vietnam: The Aftermath*. For the CD, Bang faced memories he'd tried to elude since his return home, resulting in the creation of "honest" music that allowed him to unload considerable baggage in compositions such as "Tunnel Rat (Flashlight and a .45)," a musical recollection of crawling through narrow underground tunnels dug by North Vietnamese fighters. A second CD addressing Vietnam experiences, *Vietnam: Reflections*, was released in 2005. In 2010, Bang released the emotional and critically acclaimed *A Prayer for Peace*. In the liner notes, Bang underscored his intent: "We should search for true harmony and humbleness in our lives. We should listen to each other, and be good to each other." Bang continues to perform in the United States and Europe.

Jesse Randall "J.R." "Pap" Baxter

Affectionately called "Pap" or "Pa," Jesse Randall Baxter became a champion for shape-note singing and a major force in gospel music throughout the first half of the twentieth century. Born in 1887 in Lebanon, Baxter married Clarice Howard in 1918 after a short stint as a country schoolteacher. He then took a job with T.B. Mosley and A.J. Showalter publishing company, where he learned the fundamentals of gospel harmony and music. Baxter quickly combined his teaching experience with music to teach gospel singing while developing his hymn-writing ability with such writers as James Rowe and Charles Gabriel.

Showalter soon assigned Baxter to manage the company office in Texarkana, Texas, where he met V.O. Stamps in 1926. With very different personalities, the men complemented each other professionally and became good friends, eventually forming one of the century's most successful gospel music publishing companies, the Stamps-Baxter Music and Printing Company. With Stamps as president and Baxter as vice-president, the company grew quickly, opening offices in Chattanooga, Tennessee, and Pangburn, Arkansas, publishing hymnals, operating the Stamps-Baxter School of Music and sponsoring radio programs and traveling gospel quartets, eventually becoming the world's largest gospel music business.

Baxter initially ran the Chattanooga office, but when Stamps died in 1940, he moved the company's headquarters to Dallas, Texas, where he served as general manager and president until his death on January 21, 1960. By 1943, he had written some five hundred songs. And while the Stamps-Baxter

Pap Baxter. *Courtesy of the Alabama Music Hall of Fame.*

School of Music has been credited for training several generations of singers throughout the South in composing and performing gospel music, Baxter's reach extended far beyond the school, thanks to the company's songbooks that taught shape-note singing.

Shape-note singing, or Sacred Harp singing, is a four-part harmony style derived from singers in a square facing inward, each designated to sing a specific part. Shape-note hymnals utilize note heads in four shapes, giving the style its name. Popularity in the singing style declined after World War II, and interest in gospel music shifted primarily to rural listeners. Quartets became more self-secure, no longer needing publishing companies to support them as they capitalized on the rural public's demand for entertainment. In recent years, shape-note singing has experienced a modest revival, stoked with annual Pap Baxter Heritage Gospel Singing School and Stamps-Baxter School of Music workshops, offering one- to two-week programs in the specialized style.

Stamps-Baxter Music School. *Courtesy of the Alabama Music Hall of Fame.*

Baxter is credited with authoring and/or coauthoring scores of songs that have become gospel standards, such as "Try Jesus," "Travel the Sunlit Way" and "I Want to Help Some Weary Pilgrim." Under his skilled guidance, his company boasted fifty employees by 1949, generating annual business in excess of $300,000, supporting four traveling quartets and running a Dallas school to train song leaders. After Baxter's death, his wife, "Ma" Baxter, assumed charge of the company until her death in 1972. The company was then acquired by Zondervan Publishing House in Grand Rapids, Michigan.

Blind Boys of Alabama

The Blind Boys of Alabama is one of the most enduring acts in gospel music, now entering its seventh decade. The original group—Clarence Fountain, Velma Bozman Traylor, Johnny Fields, Ollice Thomas, George Scott and J.T. Hutton, the only sighted member—formed in 1939 at the Alabama Institute for Negro Deaf and Blind, now the Alabama Institute for Deaf and Blind. The members purportedly sneaked off campus regularly to perform gospel music under the name Happy Land Jubilee Singers and found eager audiences at various military training camps throughout the South. Bolstered by clandestine popularity, the members quit school in 1945 to tour the black gospel circuit.

In 1947, under the name Happy Land Gospel Singers, the group lost lead singer Traylor to an accidental gunshot wound. The group's popularity continued to grow, though, and in 1948 in Newark, New Jersey, they performed with a group of blind singers from Mississippi known as the Jackson Harmony. Promoters hyped the event as a battle between the Blind Boys of Mississippi and the Blind Boys of Alabama. The groups adopted the names and began to tour together, capitalizing on the musical battle motif each night, with the lead singers ending shows by going down the aisles together to work crowds into a delighted frenzy. Some audience members became so excited that they succumbed to the "battle's" fervor and were taken away by ambulances.

During the mid-1950s, the Blind Boys recorded for Art Rupee's Specialty record label, but the popularity of pure gospel music waned as R&B and

The original Blind Boys of Alabama. *Courtesy of the Blind Boys of Alabama.*

rock artists incorporated gospel elements into their songs. The Blind Boys had become a leading African American gospel group by then and were determined to ride out the decline in interest. From 1963 to 1965, the group recorded on Vee Jay. In 1969, Clarence Fountain decided to pursue a solo career that didn't pan out as expected. He returned to the group in 1977.

In 1983, the pendulum of musical interest began to swing back when the group performed in *The Gospel at Colonus*, a musical version of the Sophocles play *Oedipus at Colonus*, the new version set in an African American Pentecostal church. The show won the 1984 Obie Award for best musical, and the Blind Boys' career again took off as African American gospel music experienced a revival at home and abroad. The group expanded its repertoire to include secular songs sung in gospel style, leading to the Boys' first Grammy nomination in 1992 for their cover of Bob Dylan's "I Believe in You." In 2002, *Spirit of the Century* won the Grammy for Best Traditional Gospel Album. Three subsequent albums—*Higher Ground, Go Tell It on the Mountain* and *There Will Be a Light*—also earned Best Traditional Gospel Album Grammys. The group received the Grammy Lifetime Achievement Award in 2009, along with another album Grammy for the 2008 release *Down in New Orleans*, demonstrating the Blind Boys' ability to grow and experiment, exemplified by the inclusion of jazz ensembles on various tracks.

The Blind Boys have cultivated a broad and diverse audience and appear at blues festivals, gospel celebrations and rock concerts around the world, performing gospel songs as well as secular songs by artists such as the Rolling Stones, Prince, Mahalia Jackson and Peter Gabriel. Original members Fields, Scott, Thomas and Traylor have died over the years, and Fountain no longer tours with the group due to health problems. Jimmy Carter is billed as the only original member still touring, even though the claim is slightly inaccurate. Although enrolled at the school when the group formed, he was too young to join when the Blind Boys first began touring. He did not appear on a Blind Boys record until the 1982 album *I'm a Soldier in the Army of the Lord*.

Along with Carter on vocals, the current lineup of both sighted and blind artists includes Bishop Billy Bowers, Ben Moore, Eric McKinnie, Joey Williams and Tracy Pierce. The group continues to tour and record with a variety of artists. In February 2010, the Blind Boys joined with Bob Dylan, Natalie Cole, Smokey Robinson, Seal and John Mellencamp in a performance at the White House.

Nat King Cole

To the men in the wings, a black singer—no matter who he was—had no right to perform in a white venue, and they intended to make that point clear. When he took the stage in Birmingham that night in 1956, Nathaniel Adams Cole had already become one of the century's most critically acclaimed jazz pianists and beloved voices, his notoriety rising during a time of great social and political change.

Born in Montgomery on March 17, 1919, Cole was the son of a butcher who became a Baptist minister and moved the family to Chicago when the boy was four. Cole learned piano from his mother, Perlina, and both he and his older brother Edward became professional musicians by their teens, with Cole leading two bands, the Rogues of Rhythm and the Royal Dukes. A jazz enthusiast styling himself after pianist Earl "Fatha" Hines, Cole cut his first two singles with Decca Records in 1936 with his brother's band, Eddie Cole's Swingsters. Later that year, Cole and his brother were hired to perform in the all-black Broadway revival *Shuffle Along*, where Cole met Nadine Robinson, whom he married. Only seventeen when the show closed in Los Angeles, Cole and his wife remained in California, where he began playing solo piano in clubs, including the Sewanee Inn, where owner Bob Lewis dubbed him King Cole and requested that he wear a gold paper crown during performances. Cole soon discarded the crown but retained the name. The small band he'd formed with guitarist Oscar Moore and bassist Wesley Prince became the King Cole Swingsters, later the King Cole Trio.

Nat King Cole, New York, 1947. *Photo by William P. Gottlieb, courtesy of the William P. Gottlieb/Ira and Leonore S. Gershwin Fund Collection, Music Division, Library of Congress.*

In 1941, the group's notoriety from club and radio appearances and small label recordings landed them a recording contract with Decca. By 1941, Johnny Miller had replaced Prince, and though the contract with Decca had expired, the group hit number one on *Billboard*'s Harlem Hit Parade with Cole's "That Ain't Right." Their next hit, "All for You," came from the Excelsior label in 1942, leading to a new contract with Capitol Records. Their first Capitol release, "Straighten Up and Fly Right," its lyrics based on Cole's father's sermons, topped the black chart for ten weeks and the folk chart for six and made the pop chart's Top 10, but Cole had sold all rights to the song years earlier for fifty bucks. In March 1945, *Billboard*'s first album chart ranked the King Cole Trio at number one, a position maintained for twelve weeks.

The band's recording success soon led to appearances in movies and on radio programs such as *Bing Crosby's Kraft Music Hall*, and the group hosted the show's summer replacement program in 1946. In December that year, "I Love You for Sentimental Reasons" became Cole's first number one pop single. The group then began a Saturday afternoon network radio program called *King Cole Trio Time* that ran from October 1946 through April 1948. Guitarist Irving Ashby had replaced Oscar Moore, and Cole had divorced his first wife to marry Marie Ellington. Bassist Joe Comfort replaced Johnny Miller in August 1948, and percussionist Jack Costanzo joined the group in early 1949. By 1950, the group's recordings were no longer credited to the King Cole Trio but to Nat King Cole alone. In 1950, Cole achieved his third number one pop hit with "Mona Lisa" and began near constant touring in the United States, with extended appearances at Las Vegas casinos, and trips to Europe, Asia and Latin America, shows in which he rarely played piano.

In 1951, the group officially dissolved, and Cole became a solo act, backed by guitarist John Collins, bassist Charles Harris and percussionist Costanzo. He regularly augmented the group with an orchestra. In 1953, the year Constanzo left, Cole turned to acting, taking small roles in *The Blue Gardenia*, *Small Town Girl* and the TV drama *Song for a Banjo*. That year, he also released *Nat King Cole Sings for Two in Love*, arranged and conducted by Nelson Riddle. Over the next few years, Cole released several songs, all doing well on his superstar status. As the battle for civil rights heated up, however, Cole found himself both admired and scorned by southern white audiences.

A mild-mannered man with a voice rich and beautiful, Cole garnered undesired, perhaps unwarranted, controversy. His popularity easily ranked with that of Frank Sinatra, Dean Martin and Perry Como, but his roots in jazz piano rubbed some critics and fans wrong when he made the transition to popular music. The purists condemned him for abandoning jazz, but that was minor compared to the battles he had to fight due to his race. No matter what he did, Cole found himself the target of both sides of racial issues, occasionally at the same time. Over the years, he sued numerous hotels that refused to admit him, and when he moved into an all-white Los Angeles neighborhood, racists condemned him. Then came the night of April 10, 1956.

Someone had tipped off Birmingham authorities that violence could erupt at the city's Municipal Auditorium during the much-anticipated Cole concert, so police beefed up security. African American artists had before been restricted to black establishments in the Fourth Avenue District, but times had begun to change as venues accommodated the desires of audiences. Fans packed the auditorium, while a small group of men, belonging to the White Citizens' Council movement and led by Kenneth Adams, waited in the wings. Adams was to lead a group of at least one hundred men to attack the singer and possibly kidnap him. Cole's road manager, aware of the danger, urged Cole to cancel, but Cole refused. The singer took the stage with Ted Heath and his Famous British Orchestra, the performer and band separated by a light curtain, management's attempt to soften the impact of black and white entertainers appearing together. As Cole began his third number, someone shouted, "Let's get that coon!" and four men charged the stage. A falling microphone hit the singer in the face as Adams tackled and wrestled him over a piano stool. Plainclothes policemen rushed forward, but uniformed policemen fought them back, thinking the undercover cops were a second-wave attack.

The orchestra broke into "America" (originally "God Bless the Queen") as police finally rescued Cole from the attackers. The audience sat quietly stunned until Cole returned, shaken and injured, to the stage after the arrest of his attackers. "I came here to entertain you," he told the audience. "I thought that was what you wanted. I was born here." As Mayor Jimmy Morgan and other officials rushed backstage to apologize to Cole, he reportedly said, "Man, I love show business, but I don't want to die for it." Cole returned later that night to do an uninterrupted show for an all-black audience.

Police arrested six men and discovered a cache of weapons—brass knuckles, a blackjack and a pair of .22-caliber rifles—in one of their cars. The attackers believed they would be called heroes, but the community, even some who supported segregation, responded with contempt for the Citizens' Council's use of violence. Leaving Birmingham the day after the attack, Cole cancelled upcoming shows in Charlotte and Raleigh and flew back to Chicago, where reporters asked him if he planned to continue to perform for segregated audiences. "Sure I will," he told them. "It's my job to perform for them." He said it was foolish to believe a performer could demand southern audiences to be integrated. "The Supreme Court is having a hard time integrating schools," he said. "What chance do I have to integrate audiences?" His remarks angered fans across the country, and even Thurgood Marshall quipped that "all Cole needs to complete his role as an Uncle Tom is a banjo." The criticism cut deeply, especially since Cole had waged a quiet battle against discriminatory hotels while contributing liberally to various civil rights organizations. To resolve the issue as best he could, he purchased a lifetime membership in the NAACP and vowed never to return to Alabama.

While the debacle in Birmingham and its fallout took a personal toll on Cole, it had little effect on his career. In November that year, he became the first African American to host a network series when the *Nat King Cole Show* debuted as a fifteen-minute weekly program that expanded to a half hour the following year. Although popular, the show did not attract a national

Nat King Cole and W.C. Handy. *Courtesy of the Alabama Music Hall of Fame.*

sponsor, which Cole attributed to advertisers' unwillingness to buck racial criticism. The show ended in December 1957, and Cole returned to acting, appearing in *China Gate* and *Istanbul*. In 1958, he played fellow Alabamian W.C. Handy in *St. Louis Blues*. In 1960, he put together the musical revue *I'm With You*. The show's record album hit the Top 10, but the show was unsuccessful and closed in Detroit the same year it opened. Cole salvaged the show's concept, however, and staged the production *Sights and Sounds: The Merry World of Nat King Cole*, featuring dancers and singers with whom he toured regularly from 1961 through 1964. In December 1964, as "Ramblin' Rose" reached the Top 10 and Cole completed filming for the movie *Cat Ballou*, doctors diagnosed the chain-smoking singer with lung cancer. He died on February 15, 1965, several months before *Cat Ballou*'s release.

In death as in life, Cole appeals to two separate audiences—one for his jazz performances of the 1930s and '40s and one for the popular recordings that came afterward. Critics remain split over which is his greater legacy. During his short life, he recorded more than one hundred pop chart singles and more than two dozen chart albums, ranking him second only to Sinatra as the most successful pop singer of his generation.

The Delmore Brothers

In *Truth Is Stranger than Publicity*, Alton Delmore wrote that the 1930 Old Fiddlers' Contest in Athens, Alabama, served as the turning point for him and his brother Rabon. Born the eighth and tenth children of Charlie and Mary Delmore—Alton on December 25, 1908, and Rabon on December 3, 1916—the Delmore Brothers became one of the twentieth century's most important and influential country duos.

Besides tenant farming on poor land in Limestone County, just south of the Tennessee border, the boys' father worked at a cotton mill to supplement income while the boys worked at nearby farms. In his spare time, Alton learned to read and play music, possibly from his aunt and uncle, Molly and Will Williams, enhancing the shape-note singing he'd learned at local singing schools. Encouraged by his uncle to write music, he published his first original song by age thirteen, a gospel tune called "Bound for the Shore," co-written with his mother. With guitar, fiddle and mandolin ability, Alton acquired a tenor guitar for Rabon, and the two began performing at local events and contests throughout the 1920s. Then came the Old Fiddlers' Contest in Athens. They worked their way through the various levels to the final round, playing "Columbus Stockade Blues" and "Browns Ferry Blues" as their final selections, making them the judges' unanimous winner, setting the duo on a path that would lead to the *Grand Ole Opry*.

Securing auditions with record companies and radio stations, the brothers recorded "Alabama Lullaby," backed by "Got the Kansas City Blues," for Columbia Records in 1931. The record—their only recording for

The Delmore Brothers.
Courtesy of Debby Delmore.

Columbia—sold a meager five hundred copies, but that didn't discourage them as they played any venue they could book, from schools to talent contests, always with an eye on auditioning for the *Grand Ole Opry*, the popular WSM radio country music show from Nashville. In 1933, they finally got the audition and became one of the program's most popular acts, leading to a contract with RCA. The brothers recorded more than one hundred songs on RCA's Bluebird label, with "Blues Stay Away from Me" and "Beautiful Brown Eyes" becoming hits on both the pop and country charts.

In 1938, the brothers left the *Opry*, disgruntled with management's touring restrictions, and toured the South for the next two years until signing with WAPI in Birmingham. They then recorded on the Decca label until the outbreak of World War II put their musical ambitions on hold. Alton went into the U.S. Navy, and Rabon went to work at the Wright Aircraft plant near Cincinnati, Ohio. After the war, the brothers settled in Cincinnati and revived their music career, appearing regularly on WLW radio and recording on the King label both as a solo act and with Merle Travis and Grandpa

Jones as the Browns Ferry Four, producing several gospel songs. But their exposure to the label's R&B artists inspired them to incorporate electric guitar, piano, boogie and honky-tonk into their music, taking popular music a step closer to the development of rockabilly.

Their recordings reflect an impressive ability and willingness to explore genre boundaries. Standard guitar and tenor guitar proved a successful combination for the duo's complex musical arrangements and tight harmonies. Lyrically, their songs explore the frailties of love and heartbreak and make comical observations on southern life. Their intricate harmonies softened the harder-edged sound of country music of the time and influenced duets for years to come, from the Louvin Brothers to Jim and Jesse to the Everly Brothers, while their boogie-influenced tunes inspired the growth of honky-tonk and rockabilly during the 1950s.

Despite their innovations and general popularity, superstardom never came. In 1950, Alton suffered a heart attack. In 1951, the brothers' father died. In 1952, Alton's three-year-old daughter died, and doctors diagnosed Rabon with lung cancer. After Rabon's death that December, Alton moved to Huntsville to take a job with the U.S. Postal Service while teaching music on the side, writing short fiction and working on his autobiography. He died on June 9, 1964, of heart failure.

Among their many honors, the Delmore Brothers have been inducted into the Nashville Songwriters Hall of Fame, the Alabama Music Hall of Fame and the Country Music Hall of Fame. Interest in their music remains high as their songs continue to be covered by artists such as Doc Watson, k.d. lang and Mark Knopfler.

Cleveland Eaton

His bass work is legendary, from his career as a solo artist to his work with artists such as the Ramsey Lewis Trio and Count Basie Orchestra. Cleveland Josephus Eaton II, born in Fairfield on August 31, 1939, got his first close look at an upright acoustic bass the day his high school band teacher brought one to class. Eaton had been studying music since age five—first piano and then trumpet and saxophone—but when high school band teacher John Springer allowed him to take the bass home, he was hooked and eventually mastered the instrument to become one of the best-known and most versatile jazz bassists in the business.

After earning a BA in music in 1960 at Tennessee A&I State University, Eaton moved to Chicago to join the Ike Cole Trio and then the Ramsey Lewis Trio, appearing on more than thirty recordings with four singles and four albums reaching gold. He then became "the Count's Bassist," spending sixteen years with the Count Basie Orchestra, branching into composition, arrangement and eventually into production and publishing to head his own Birmingham-based record company. Since 1974, he has also toured with his own group, Cleave Eaton and Co. In 1985, he turned to teaching as well, creating the UA–Birmingham jazz ensemble even as he continued to work with his own band.

Despite his many years and experiences playing for people around the country and world, Eaton cites as one of his favorite memories a single gig in Birmingham's Ensley suburb during the civil rights movement. As the time to go onstage approached, some feared that an integrated audience could lead to trouble, especially in Alabama's volatile protest days. But Eaton insisted that

Cleveland Eaton. *Photo by Richard Manoske, courtesy of the Birmingham (Alabama) Public Library.*

jazz audiences were above the fracas because jazz itself was an integrated world. And he was right, at least that night, with not one adverse incident reported.

In 2004, he changed the name of his group to Cleave Eaton and the Alabama All Stars, composed of trumpeter Tommy Stewart, saxophonists Gary Wheat and Dave Amaral, drummer John Nuckols, trombonist Chad Fisher, guitarist Carlos Pino and pianist Ray Reach. Over the years, Eaton has performed with the greatest names in American music, from Miles Davis and Sarah Vaughn to Dizzy Gillespie, Ella Fitzgerald and the Temptations. He's earned numerous awards, including Canada's Cultural Enhancement Award, the Don Redman Lifetime Achievement Award and the Alabama Governor's Arts Award. In 2008, he was inducted into the Alabama Music Hall of Fame.

In 2009, doctors diagnosed Eaton with oral cancer, but the cancer responded well to treatment. By 2011, he was cancer free and accepting donations through his website to help defray the exorbitant medical costs for treatment. Eaton continues to perform with his and other bands, bringing audiences together with music that defies boundaries.

Eric Essix

In December 2009, jazz guitarist Eric Essix gave some love back to Birmingham, putting on a show to celebrate the town of his birth fifty years earlier. With trumpeter Joey Sommerville and violinist Michael Ward, Essix marked a milestone in his life, demonstrating that success in the music business doesn't always necessitate leaving the home you love. Born on December 29, 1959, Essix began his musical journey at age ten when his grandfather bought him his first electric guitar and amp. He quickly taught himself to play well enough to perform with church groups and to compete in high school talent contests, all the while developing and refining a style that would define him as one of contemporary jazz's most gifted and respected guitarists.

The Beatles—as they were for many artists growing up in the 1960s—proved one of Essix's earliest musical influences. Their 1964 and 1965 appearances on the *Ed Sullivan Show* made a lasting impression on the young Essix, and by the time his grandfather gave him the guitar, he was eager to learn and play his own music. Essix taught himself to play by listening to and accompanying albums by the Beatles, Stevie Wonder, Al Green and others. He was also deeply impressed by the hard rock style of Jimi Hendrix. His exposure to jazz, though, was limited, his first experience being Wes Montgomery's 1966 album, *California Dreaming*. Then came a 1977 Weather Report concert. The group's ability to intertwine jazz and rock elements into intricate instrumentals affected Essix so profoundly that he decided to specialize in instrumental jazz.

Eric Essix.
*Photo by Cameron
Carnes and Taylor
Christian, courtesy
of Eric Essix.*

His first solo album, *First Impressions,* released in 1988, landed him a deal with Los Angeles–based Nova Records, where he produced *Second Thoughts,* which delivered the national hits "Come September" and "First Out." His next release, *Third Degree Burn,* came in 1993 after he graduated from Boston's Berklee College of Music. The two-year promotional tour for *Third Degree Burn* resulted in the live album *Essix & Modern Man Live!* In 1998 and 2000 on the Zebra label, Essix topped the smooth jazz radio charts with "For Real" from the album *Small Talk* and scored a Top 10 hit with "Rainy Night in Georgia" from *Southbound.*

In 2002, Essix joined the trend of artists leaving their labels to go independent. He formed Essential Recordings, based in Birmingham, and began distributing his music online through download sites such as iTunes. Essix's love for his hometown is evident in his musical journey back to Birmingham, beginning with his roots-based release *Southbound* in 2000, followed by *Somewhere in Alabama* and *Birmingham.* After touring as a sideman for several acts that included Steve Cole and Jeff Kashiwa in 2006, he founded the Preserve Jazz Festival in Hoover, Alabama, in 2007, featuring major jazz acts on the first Sunday in June each year.

In 2009, he returned to the studio to record the CD *Superblue,* backed by the Night Flight Big Band, with guest saxophonist Lou Marini, a veteran of the *Saturday Night Live* and Blues Brothers bands. Even though his duties have grown to encompass business management and record production, Essix maintains that his greatest joy comes from playing guitar with other musicians, whether it's onstage or in the studio. "There is nothing else that comes close."

Eddie Floyd

S tax Records is legendary for producing such artists as Otis Redding, Albert King, Booker T. and the MGs and Isaac Hayes, but Eddie Floyd proved one of the company's best assets, not only for producing and recording multiple hits but also for writing songs that transformed other Stax artists into stars. Floyd was born on June 25, 1937, in Montgomery and later moved to Detroit, Michigan, with his immediate family but lived alternately with relatives in Alabama and Detroit, receiving a more diverse musical experience by spending much of his youth in two different states.

As Floyd's interests led him toward a music career, it certainly helped to have his uncle Robert West already in the business as the founder of the Lupine and Flick record labels, two early rivals to Motown Record Corporation. Floyd's uncle proved an excellent asset in the 1950s when he negotiated a contract with Mercury Records for Floyd's racially integrated group the Falcons. As the group began to garner moderate success in 1959, however, its two white singers, Bob Manardo and Tom Shelter, left for military service, and the Falcons became an all–African American group, featuring Joe Stubbs, Willie Schoefield, Bonny "Mack" Rice, Lance Fannie and Floyd. Their first hit, "You're So Fine," with Stubbs on lead vocals, reached the pop chart's Top 20, but following songs didn't do as well until Wilson Pickett replaced Stubbs and recorded "I Found a Love" with the group backed by the Primettes, an early incarnation of the Supremes. Pickett didn't stay long, though, leaving in 1963 to pursue a solo career. By then, Floyd was weary of the group as well, and the Falcons disbanded.

Eddie Floyd. *Photo by and courtesy of Simon Tainton, SIMpixels Photography.*

Floyd spent time with his uncle's label, recording singers such as Mary Wilson and Dianna Ross, until he decided to move to Washington, D.C., to form the Safice label with Moonglows member Chester Simmons and disc jockey Al Bell. Although the label struck a distribution deal with Atlantic, Bell and Floyd soon left, and Floyd moved to Memphis to join Stax Records in 1965 as a songwriter and producer. One of his first efforts, "Knock on Wood," co-written with Steve Cropper, went to number twenty-eight on the charts. By 1970, Floyd had recorded twelve songs that charted in the Top 100, including "I've Never Found a Girl (to Love Me Like You Do)" and a cover of "Bring It on Home to Me." While recording on his own, Floyd also wrote for others, including the hit he co-wrote with Steve Cropper for Wilson Pickett, "634-5789."

Penning hits for artists as diverse as Solomon Burke, Sam & Dave, Johnnie Taylor, Albert King and Rufus Thomas, Floyd earned the reputation that he could write songs for any artist. Pairing with Booker T. Jones, Floyd co-wrote several songs that did as well as those he'd written with Cropper, including "I Love You More than Words Can Say" for Otis Redding, who died in a plane crash in 1967 while Floyd was on tour in England. As he waited in a British airport for a flight back to the United States, Floyd wrote "Big Bird" in honor of Redding.

By the 1970s, Floyd had moved to California to continue work with Jones while still working with Stax, releasing songs as good as any previously released, but mounting legal and financial problems prevented Stax from promoting the work properly. Floyd learned the depth of Stax's problems on December 19, 1975, when his two-year-old daughter found his pistol and accidentally shot herself. When Floyd called Stax's Memphis office to get details of his medical insurance, he was told that he'd have to wait because federal marshals were closing the place down. Luckily, his daughter survived.

During the 1980s, Floyd released an album on Seasaint Records, which led to his recruitment by the newly reformed Booker T. and the MGs and then the Blues Brothers Band. He appeared in the 1998 movie *Blues Brothers 2000* and continued to make guest appearances with the Blues Brothers Band into the twenty-first century. In 2002, he received the Memphis Sound award, and in January 2003, performing his hits "634-5789" and "I've Never Found a Girl (to Love Me Like You Do)" to an appreciative Alabama crowd, he was inducted into the Alabama Music Hall of Fame. Since then, he's toured Europe with the Blues Brothers Band, appeared in Spain with B.B. King and toured Europe and the United Kingdom with former Rolling Stones bassist Bill Wyman. In 2008, he released the album *Eddie Loves You* for LA-based Concord Records.

William Christopher Handy

He's known as the "Father of the Blues," but some suggest he might be more aptly called the "Transcriber of the Blues." William Christopher Handy was born in Florence to former slaves on November 16, 1873, eight years after the end of the Civil War. With wages secreted under slavery, his father purchased farmland in Florence following the war and worked as both a farmer and a minister of the African Methodist Episcopal Church. Handy's early musical education came from hymns and spirituals as he played the harmonium in his father's church and from folk and popular tunes he learned from itinerant fiddler Whit Walker.

Growing up on the farm, Handy found nature a prime source for music, claiming later that he'd learned melody by listening to birds and other animals. His compositions, however, suggest more interest in the minstrel shows that passed through Florence, featuring cakewalks and popular marches. By age sixteen, Handy had begun arranging popular songs into four-part harmony to sing with friends from school. After earning a teaching certificate from Huntsville Teachers Agricultural and Mechanical College in 1892, Handy shunned teaching for a better-paying job at Bessemer Iron Works outside Birmingham. He earned extra money by performing with the vocal Lauzetta Quartet and teaching musicians how to read notes. His quartet decided to attend the Chicago World's Fair in 1892, working jobs along the way. But when they arrived, they learned the fair had been postponed a year, so they decided to go to St. Louis, where they found little work and eventually disbanded. The folksongs that Handy heard in St.

W.C. Handy. *Courtesy of the Alabama Music Hall of Fame.*

Louis, though, would later provide the basis for his most famous piece, "St. Louis Blues."

Handy soon moved to Evansville, Indiana, where he joined a band that performed throughout neighboring states. From 1893 through 1896, he honed his cornet skills by playing in various brass bands. He also met Elizabeth Price, whom he married in 1896. The couple would eventually have six children. Later that year, he joined the Mahara Minstrels for a three-year tour that wound through the South and to Cuba. As the tour returned north and passed through Alabama, Handy and Elizabeth decided to take a break and stayed in Florence. Handy accepted a position to teach at the Agricultural and Mechanical College, a job that didn't last long because he decided to rejoin the Mahara Minstrels to tour the Midwest and Pacific Northwest. He left the show again in 1903, this time to direct the Knights of Pythias in Clarksdale, Mississippi, where he became fully immersed in the blues. He traveled the region extensively, learning and writing down melodies and lyrics sung by artists in the emerging Mississippi blues style until 1909, when he moved the Knights to Memphis.

Most biographers point to Handy's time in Mississippi as the period that defined him as the "Father of the Blues." But rather than invent the blues, Handy set the style to paper and made it palatable to both black and white audiences. The blues style dates back to the 1800s, and even in Memphis, the Charlie Bynum & Jim Turner Band, not Handy, proved the first to play the blues on Beale Street. But it was Handy who realized the commercial potential of scoring songs in the blues style, and he capitalized on the opportunity.

In 1913, Handy and Harry Pace, a young businessman from Covington, Georgia, founded the Pace & Handy Music Company in Memphis, publishing what would become known as Handy's masterpiece, "St. Louis Blues," in 1914. Although it would become one of the twentieth century's biggest hits, it made little impact at the time it was published. Some historians and reviewers believe the eventual success of "St. Louis Blues" may be due more to Handy's close association with the New York recording industry than the piece's musical appeal. Whatever the case, "St. Louis Blues" and the songs that followed have secured Handy's place in history. "St. Louis Blues" was not Handy's first blues song, however. His first came in 1909 as a composition for Memphis mayoral candidate E.H. Crump, initially entitled "Mr. Crump." The song later became the successful "Memphis Blues" when it was published in 1912.

In 1918, Handy established Handy Brothers Music Company in New York and began compiling blues tunes for the collection *Blues: An Anthology: Complete Words and Music of 53 Great Songs*, which he published in 1926. Books that followed included the *Book of Negro Spirituals*, *Negro Authors and Composers of the United States*, *Unsung Americans Sung* and his autobiography, *Father of the Blues*.

In the 1930s, Handy's vision began to deteriorate. In 1937, his wife died. In 1943, he lost his sight completely when he fell from a subway station platform. Eleven years later, at the age of eighty, he married Irma Louise Logan. Within a year, a stroke confined him to a wheelchair, and he died on March 28, 1958, of pneumonia. He was buried in Woodlawn Cemetery, Bronx, New York, as an estimated 150,000 people lined the funeral route. Shortly after Handy's death, Nat King Cole starred as Handy in the loosely biographical movie *St. Louis Blues*. In 1969, the U.S. Postal Service issued a stamp in his honor. Other posthumous awards include induction into the Alabama Music Hall of Fame, Nashville Songwriters Hall of Fame, Alabama Jazz Hall of Fame and National Academy of Popular Music Songwriters

Hall of Fame. The log cabin in which he was born has been restored into a museum, and each year Florence holds an annual music festival in his honor. The Handy Brothers Music Company, one of the oldest family-owned African American businesses in New York, continues to operate.

Emmylou Harris

E mmylou Harris is impossible to pigeonhole, her influence broad and remarkable. She's considered one of the most distinctive recording personalities of the last half century, her music spanning several genres. And she's even credited with helping to revive country music with the songs and traditions on which it was built while at the same time introducing new songwriters whose work conveys the same authenticity as that of traditional artists.

Born April 2, 1947, in Birmingham, Harris moved to Cherry Point, North Carolina, with her family at age six. Because of her father's frequent transfers in the U.S. Marines, the family soon moved again, this time to Quantico, Virginia, and then to Woodbridge, where she later won the Miss Woodbridge beauty pageant. When she was sixteen, her maternal grandfather gave her a Kay guitar he bought from a pawnshop for thirty bucks, whetting her musical appetite. After graduating as class valedictorian from Gar-Field High School, she won a dramatic scholarship to the University of North Carolina, where she studied theater and developed an interest in folk music, learning songs by Bob Dylan and Joan Baez.

Harris began playing in local clubs with fellow student Mike Williams and eventually dropped out of college to move to New York to pursue a career in folk music, even though its popularity had begun to wane. She played the Greenwich Village club circuit, occasionally sharing the stage and becoming friends with performers such as David Bromberg and Paul Siebel. Night gigs didn't pay much, though, and she had to supplement her income by working

Emmylou Harris. *Photo by and courtesy of Eric Frommer.*

as a waitress and bookstore clerk while living at the YWCA. In 1969, she married Tom Slocum and signed with a struggling folk label that released her album *Gliding Bird* in 1970. Shortly after the album's release, and with Harris pregnant, the company declared bankruptcy as her marriage began to dissolve.

Divorcing Slocum and committing to rear their daughter, Hallie, alone, Harris moved to Nashville in search of a career break that didn't come, forcing her to move in with her parents who had bought a farm outside Washington, D.C. Harris soon formed a trio in D.C. with Gerry Mule and Tom Guidera to perform in area clubs, and that's where her breakthrough finally came in 1971, when former Byrds members Chris Hillman and Gram Parsons heard her perform in a small nightclub. Parsons asked her to join him in Los Angeles in 1972 to work on his first solo album, *GP*. In 1973,

Parsons died from a drug overdose, and Harris returned to D.C., drawing from members of the Gram Parsons band to form a country band that helped her land her first record deal on a major label, Reprise Records. She released *Pieces in the Sky* in 1975, composed mostly of covers ranging from the Beatles to the Louvin Brothers and containing what would become one of her most famous songs, "Boulder to Birmingham," a hauntingly emotional farewell to Parsons.

The album's producer, Brian Ahern, produced Harris's next ten records and became her second husband. For her second album, 1976's *Elite Hotel*, Harris again featured covers of songs by a variety of artists from Patsy Cline to Buck Owens, with her versions of Owens's "Together Again" and Cline's "Sweet Dreams" topping the charts. She then recorded with Bob Dylan for *Desire* and appeared in Martin Scorsese's documentary on the Band, *The Last Waltz*. Then came *Luxury Liner* in 1977 and *Quarter Moon in a Ten-Cent Town* in 1978. Eventually, her marriage to Ahern fell apart, and she returned with her children, Hallie and Meghann, to Nashville, where she began work with Paul Kennerley, who became her third husband, on *The Ballad of Sally Rose*. It proved a commercial failure when released in 1985.

In 1987, she teamed with Dolly Parton and Linda Ronstadt to record *Trio*, a collection of songs that became one of her bestselling albums to date. And though she's established herself as an extraordinary songwriter, she may be better known for her ability to reinterpret other artists' songs. In 1993, she moved to Asylum Records, releasing *Cowgirl's Prayer* shortly after her separation from Kennerley. In 1995, her album *Wrecking Ball* surprised many critics with another departure from what might have been expected based on what had come before. Pairing Harris with singers such as Neil Young for songs by Gillian Welch, Steve Earle and Julie Miller, producer Daniel Lanois guided her into alternative country.

In 1999, Harris began lending her celebrity and talents to political and social issues that included work with People for the Ethical Treatment of Animals (PETA) and Concerts for a Landmine Free World, benefiting the Vietnam Veterans of America Foundation. Since 2000, she's teamed with numerous artists, including the Chieftains, Mark Knopfler, John Prine, Dixie Chicks, Tracy Chapman and Delbert McClinton. Harris has received many honors, including a dozen Grammys, *Billboard*'s Century Award (1999) and induction into the Country Music Hall of Fame and Alabama Music Hall of Fame. She currently lives in Nashville.

Odetta Holmes

She was a champion of folk music, a living archive of songs, singing with extraordinary power and clarity while drawing on a variety of musical genres to influence such renowned singers as Janis Joplin and Joan Armatrading. Born on December 31, 1930, in Birmingham, Odetta Holmes, who chose to use only her first name throughout her career, became one of the most influential folk musicians of the twentieth century.

Odetta's father died when she was young. Her mother remarried when the girl was six and changed the children's surname to their stepfather's name, Felious. The family moved to Los Angeles, where they encountered segregation similar to that in Alabama. Despite living within walking distance of Marshall High School, Odetta was bused farther away to Belmont High School. Taking voice and piano lessons, she became the star of her high school glee club and began appearing by age fourteen with the Madrigal Singers at Hollywood's Turnabout Theater. She appeared to be destined for a career as a classical singer, but she realized the genre would limit her options for success. She decided to branch into other forms of music and landed a chorus member part in a production of *Finian's Rainbow*. During the play's San Francisco run, she met up with an old friend who introduced her to folksongs, and she became enamored with the style. She bought a guitar, learned some chords and began singing at parties, later crediting the early songs for helping her to work through what she called "hate and fury" without being antisocial. She cherished the songs for providing a fresh and honest view of history—especially African American history—that school had not provided.

Odetta. *Photo by and courtesy of M. Joseph de Oliveira.*

Odetta began performing at folk clubs in San Francisco in 1950 and recorded her first album, *The Tin Angel*, in 1954, drawing attention from such folk icons as Pete Seeger, Woody Guthrie and Jack Elliot. Writing and performing on the old acoustic she nicknamed "Baby," Odetta never considered herself much of a guitarist, but she developed a unique style that eventually became known as the "Odetta strum." In the right place and the right time, with the right sound and appeal, Odetta became one of the primary stars of the folk music renaissance in the late 1950s and early 1960s, using TV adeptly to reach an ever-broadening audience on shows such as the *Tennessee Ernie Ford Show* and specials such as 1963's *Dinner with the President*. She played the Newport Folk Festival four times between 1959 and 1965, appeared at Carnegie Hall in 1961 and secured a recording contract with Vanguard Records, the leader in folk music at the time. With a repertoire of songs that ranged from nineteenth-century slave songs and spirituals to songs by Guthrie and Seeger, Odetta ultimately influenced such artists as Bob Dylan, Tracy Chapman and Joan Baez.

Odetta later branched into movie and television acting, taking roles in films that included *The Autobiography of Miss Jane Pittman* and *Sanctuary*. Folk music, however, remained her passion. She preferred to appear solo in concert so she could tailor her music to the specific audience. "I'm not a purist in any way, shape, or form," she once said about her style. "If I felt I needed to sing a song so badly and I couldn't play accompaniment for it, I would sing it a cappella." She insisted, "The folk repertoire is our inheritance. Don't have to like it, but we need to hear it." She made it her life's mission to bring that music to younger generations, to offer them an alternative to the homogenized, overproduced music that chokes radio airwaves today.

Thrice married and twice divorced, Odetta constantly researched traditional forms of music through the Library of Congress and eagerly added the styles to her repertoire. "As long as I am performing," she told one interviewer, "I will be pointing out that heritage that is ours." In 1965, at the height of the civil rights movement, Birmingham officials presented her with the key to the city in recognition of her accomplishments. In 1999, President Bill Clinton awarded her the National Medal of Arts. In 2004, she was a Kennedy Center honoree, and the Library of Congress honored her in 2005 with its Living Legend Award.

Despite failing health, Odetta performed more than sixty concerts during 2007 and 2008. In November 2008, she entered New York City's Lenox Hill Hospital for a checkup related to heart disease but suffered kidney failure and had to remain hospitalized. Having performed "I'm on My Way" at the historic August 1963 March on Washington the day Martin Luther King delivered the "I Have a Dream" speech, she had been invited to perform at Barack Obama's presidential inauguration in January 2009. She continued to prepare for and looked forward to performing at the inauguration, but on December 3, 2008, she succumbed. Although her voice graced many styles of music—jazz, show tunes, opera—Odetta will forever be remembered for her massive repertoire of traditional American folk music and her commitment to social justice.

Sonny James

S onny James, the celebrated "Southern Gentleman," spent more time on the charts at number one than any other country artist—a total of fifty-seven weeks between 1960 and 1979. Born in Hackleburg on May 1, 1929, James Loden became part of a musical family that operated a three-hundred-acre farm supported by three tenant families who worked cooperatively to raise cotton, hay and corn. James's parents immersed their children in music, exposing them to a variety of performers via the family's Victrola and radio while teaching them to play various instruments. James caught on quickly and was performing in the family band by age three.

In 1933, the family band auditioned for WMSD in Muscle Shoals, earning themselves a regular Saturday slot. By 1936, the Lodens had developed a following throughout the South, convincing James's father that the band should turn professional. They soon secured a slot on KCLN in Blytheville, Arkansas, a station that reached three states. The Lodens spent the next two years building a solid reputation for the ability to play songs from pop to country, fueling demand for them as an opening act for headliners. Just before World War II, the band landed a spot on Knoxville's WNOX, playing the daily *Midday Merry-Go-Round* and Saturday night's *Tennessee Barn Dance*.

In 1946, they moved to WPTF in Raleigh, North Carolina, where James met and regularly jammed with two musicians who worked in Johnny and Jack's Tennessee Mountain Boys, fiddler Paul Warren and guitarist Chet Atkins. Three years later, the Lodens returned to Alabama for a slot on Birmingham's WSGN, followed by a move to Memphis's WMPS. Two of

Sonny James (rear left) and family. *Courtesy of the Alabama Music Hall of Fame.*

the sisters married and left the act soon after the move to Memphis, and the group, failing to find adequate replacement musicians, eventually dissolved. Hardly any of the group's performances were recorded, and though they could have enjoyed wider popularity, they had refused to perform in bars and nightclubs, limiting themselves to the radio circuit, a habit that James retained as a solo artist.

Following the band's demise, James contacted friend Freddy Burns, who fronted a band featured on a noontime show on Memphis's WHBQ that fed to stations on the Mutual Broadcasting System. Burns invited James to join him, and James spent the next summer playing fiddle for Burns's band, which led to his own daily quarter-hour show in which he performed with a bassist. Having joined the National Guard while in high school, James's stint at the station ended in 1950 when his unit was placed on active duty. By year's end, he was in Korea.

James maintained his musicianship with an inexpensive guitar and fiddle during his Korean deployment, and he was eager to start performing again when he returned to Alabama in 1952. He contacted his old jamming partner, Chet Atkins, now an established session musician and regularly featured on the Prince Albert segment of the *Grand Ole Opry*. Impressed with James's intimate style and songs, Atkins introduced him to Capitol producer Ken Nelson, and a recording deal was struck. Nelson also convinced James to adopt the stage name "Sonny James," and though James balked at first, he agreed, only to have Nelson further brand him as the "Southern Gentleman."

For the first recording session in June 1952, Nelson selected four songs that James had written during his time in Korea. "That's Me Without You" made the country Top 10 in 1953, but James didn't have another hit until "For Rent (One Empty Heart)" climbed to number seven on the country chart three years later. The year 1956 was also the one for his biggest hit, "Young Love," which stayed at number one for nine weeks and became a pop hit as well. After the success of "Young Love," James focused on giving his country songs a more pop sound. In the 1960s, that "sound" produced a multiyear run of number one singles, with twenty-one of twenty-five rising to the country chart's top position for a total of forty-five weeks. To enhance his success, James used television to its promotional potential, appearing on the *Ed Sullivan Show*, *Hee Haw* and the *Bob Hope Show*, while also appearing in several movies, including *Las Vegas Hillbillies*, *Nashville Rebel* and *Second Fiddle to a Steel Guitar*.

James had another run of Top 10 hits during the 1970s, but it couldn't rival his string of number ones during the 1960s. His last number one hit came in 1974 with "Is It Wrong (for Loving You)," but by then he had expanded his talents into producing and publishing, working with artists that included Marie Osmond. By the time he retired to Nashville in 1983, James had recorded seventy-two chart hits. James has received numerous career-associated honors, including a star on the Hollywood Walk of Fame in 1971 and induction into the Alabama Music Hall of Fame in 1987, Country Music Hall of Fame in 2006 and Hit Parade Hall of Fame in 2009. He received the Career Achievement Award from the Country Music DJ Hall of Fame in 2002.

Eddie Kendrick,
Paul Williams and
Melvin Franklin

A t Fourth Avenue North and Eighteenth Street, near Birmingham's Sixteenth Street Baptist Church, where four young girls died in 1963 in a racially motivated bombing, the Eddie Kendrick Memorial Park honors one of the most famous soul and pop groups ever to record—the Temptations. The memorial, sculpted by Ronald Scott McDowell, depicts the original Temptations in dance moves that helped establish the group as one of pop music's most successful.

Union Springs native Eddie Kendrick grew up in Birmingham's Tuxedo Junction area, where he met Birmingham native Paul Williams in their church choir. Both born in 1939, the two men formed the Cavaliers with friends Kel Osborn and Jerome Averette to perform secular music. They moved to Cleveland, Ohio, in 1957 and then to Detroit, where they changed their name to the Primes, but the group disbanded when Osborn left to pursue a solo career. Kendrick added an *s* to his name around the time he and Williams met Montgomery native Melvin Franklin (born David English in 1942). Thanks to his deep, rich voice, Franklin had signed a contract with Motown Records by age thirteen and established a notable reputation in the Voicemasters by 1959. While in high school, he and Otis Williams, with whom he formed a friendship that lasted the rest of their lives, became members of the Distants. He met Kendricks and Williams when they joined the group on invitation from Otis Williams. By 1960, the Distants had become the Elgins, with Eldridge Bryant rounding

The Eddie Kendrick Memorial, Birmingham. *Photo by C.S. Fuqua.*

out the group. Within a year, they had signed with Motown under the name the Temptations.

The group debuted on Motown's Gordy Records label in 1962 with "Oh, Mother of Mine," but their first four songs flopped. Choreographer Cholly Atkins then came in to improve the group's stage presence, but tension between members surfaced, and Bryant left and was replaced by David Ruffin. Reenergized, with Kendricks now on lead vocals, the group hit solid in 1964 with "The Way You Do the Things You Do," which reached number eleven. In 1965, they captured number one on both the pop and R&B charts with Smokey Robinson's "My Girl," followed by "It's Growing," "Since I Lost My Baby," "Get Ready," "Ain't Too Proud to Beg" and "I Know I'm Losing You."

Kendricks and Ruffin began sharing lead vocals while Kendricks wrote some of the group's songs, including "Isn't She Pretty" and "No Man Can Love Her Like I Do." Kendricks sang lead on "Just My Imagination (Running Away With Me)," which reached number one on the pop and R&B charts in 1971. He then left to pursue a solo career, backed by the Young Senators, finding success with disco hits such as "Keep on Truckin'" and "Boogie Down." In 1978, Kendricks left Motown for Arista Records and had hits with "Ain't No Smoke Without Fire" and "I Just Want to Be the One in Your Life."

Reverting to his name's original spelling, Kendrick reunited with the Temptations in 1982 to tour in promotion of their hit "Standing at the Top." Kendrick and Ruffin then teamed up to record "I Couldn't Believe It" in 1987 and "One More for the Lonely Hearts Club" in 1988. In 1991, Ruffin died of a drug overdose, and doctors diagnosed Kendrick with lung cancer, removing the affected lung in an attempt to stop the spread. As Kendrick's health improved, he sued Motown for allegedly withholding royalties. That summer, he toured Europe and Japan, but the cancer returned, and he died at home in Birmingham on October 5, 1992, before the lawsuit could be settled. Kendrick had no health insurance, leaving his family facing enormous medical costs that Bobby Womack helped to defray by organizing two benefit concerts. Kendrick is buried in Birmingham's Elmwood Cemetery.

The Temptations' "heart and soul," Paul Williams, faced a mountain of financial and emotional problems by 1969, with alcohol dependency devastating his health. In 1971, he left the group but stayed in touch with members while producing the solo release "Feel Like Givin' Up." On August 17, 1973, he was found dead, shot in the head and lying in a Detroit alley beside his car. Authorities ruled the death a suicide, but his family questioned that ruling because Williams, according to the coroner, had shot himself in the left side of the head using his right hand. The gun itself had been fired twice, but only one shot had hit Williams. A bottle of whiskey was on the ground near his body's left side, as though he'd dropped it.

Melvin Franklin's rich voice had always delighted Temptations audiences, especially when he sang "Ol' Man River" from *Showboat*. Franklin had an absorbing and kind personality and received the Motown Spirit Award several times in recognition of his grace. Although "Ol' Man River" was an audience favorite, his trademark was the line "and the band played on" from the Temptations hit "Ball of Confusion." In the late 1960s, doctors diagnosed Franklin with rheumatoid arthritis and later with diabetes. By 1993, Franklin had grown so ill that he required wheelchair assistance to and from stage and supplemental oxygen backstage during performance breaks. In 1994, he became too ill to perform. On February 17, 1995, a series of seizures resulted in a six-day coma before he succumbed to heart failure in Los Angeles's Cedars-Sinai Hospital.

The Temptations are one of Motown's most enduring and popular acts, wowing audiences with a mix of songs and styles set to precisely executed choreography. Their many awards include induction into the Rock and Roll Hall of Fame in 1989, NAACP Hall of Fame in 1992 and Vocal Group Hall of Fame in 1999. With forty-nine albums to their credit, the Temptations continued to tour in 2011 with a lineup that included only one original member, Otis Williams.

The Louvin Brothers

The 1950s proved an evolutionary period in popular music, thanks to performers like the Louvin Brothers. Ira and Charlie Loudermilk were born in Henagar on April 21, 1924, and July 7, 1927, respectively, two of seven children in a family that raised cotton, vegetables and sugar cane on twenty-three acres. Their exposure to music came early. Their father was a banjo picker and fiddler, and their mother was a shape-note singer. Church involvement exposed the brothers to hymns, while their father's record collection and the *Grand Ole Opry* exposed them to artists such as Roy Acuff, the Delmore Brothers and Uncle Dave Macon. Influenced most by Bill Monroe, Ira gave his guitar to Charlie and bought his first mandolin at age nineteen. When they began to perform, they adopted the name the Louvin Brothers because others joked about Loudermilk and found it difficult to spell.

Although they had begun to perform publicly but not professionally, the brothers nearly ended the act due to a 1938 fire that destroyed the family home, Ira's first of four marriages and the birth of his daughter and Ira's move to Chattanooga, Tennessee, to take a cotton mill job to support his family. But Charlie decided to move to Chattanooga as well, and the brothers continued to work on new songs. Their first professional gig came in Flat Rock, Alabama, at the 1941 Fourth of July celebration, where they played at the event's flying jenny, a mule-powered merry-go-round. They played two songs per ride and earned two dollars each for the gig.

In 1942, three consecutive wins of a weekly amateur contest in Chattanooga netted the grand prize of playing a fifteen-minute radio show

The Louvin Brothers. *Courtesy of Steele Management.*

each day at 4:30 a.m., after which they worked their day jobs and played music at night at area venues. In 1945, Charlie joined the army and Ira moved to Knoxville, where he joined Charlie Monroe's band. The army discharged Charlie in 1946, and Ira quit Monroe's band to reunite musically with his brother in Memphis, where they stayed for the next four years, performing three shows a day on WMPS and playing area gigs at night. They cut their first commercial records for the Apollo Records label during this time, catching the attention of Nashville song publisher Fred Rose, who had connections with such stars as Hank Williams and Roy Acuff.

By 1949, Charlie had married, and the brothers, unable to bring in enough money with music, took jobs at the Memphis Post Office while continuing to play nights and weekends. They also recorded a single for Decca Records, but it failed to make an impact. By the end of the year, they had signed a contract with MGM Records, and they recorded twelve songs over the next twelve months. The brothers then signed with Capitol Records, where they recorded the moderately successful "The Family Who Prays" and several other gospel songs, including "Weapon of Prayer" and "Satan Is Real."

Musical Heritage from the Heart of Dixie

In 1953, Charlie was recalled by the army and sent to Korea. Upon his return home in 1954, the brothers took up where they'd left off, touring and recording, displaying particular attention to harmonies. In 1955, the *Grand Ole Opry* hired them, and they began recording country songs, including the hit "When I Stop Dreaming." Within the next five years, ten songs reached the Top 10, including "I Don't Believe You've Met My Baby," which hit number one. Although secular songs proved successful, they continued to record gospel songs as well, updating the sound to reflect current musical trends.

While the brother act experienced greater success, Ira's personal life, especially his problems with alcohol, grew over the years until Charlie could accept it no longer, and the act disbanded in 1963. Ira recorded a few records afterward, but he wasn't able to generate much interest. In June 1965, he and his fourth wife, Florence, who performed as Anne Young, died in an automobile accident on Father's Day, en route home following a tour of Missouri with other performers. Unlike Ira, Charlie enjoyed a successful solo career, recording hits that included "See the Big Man Cry, Mama" and "I Don't Love You Anymore." In the 1970s, he recorded several duets with Melba Montgomery.

The Louvin Brothers are considered vital to the transformation of country music from a regional, rural genre into a national genre after World War II. Their gospel songs are considered some of the twentieth century's lyrically best, while their secular songs remain as poignant today as they were when first recorded. Their music has influenced numerous artists, including Jim and Jesse, Johnny Cash and Emmylou Harris. Among their many awards, the brothers have been inducted into the Songwriters Hall of Fame, Alabama Music Hall of Fame and Country Music Hall of Fame.

Charlie continued a heavy performance schedule through the decades into the twenty-first century. In November 2010 at age eighty-three, he released his last album, *The Battles Rage On*, a collection of war songs dating back to the American Civil War. The excitement of the new album, however, was dampened by the discovery five months earlier that he had developed pancreatic cancer. Doctors had hoped to correct the problem through surgery but failed, and Charlie began alternative treatment. In late October, several artists, including Alison Krauss, held a benefit show in Bell Buckle, Tennessee, to raise more than $20,000 to help Charlie counter mounting medical bills. David Boley, representative of the Foggy Hollow Bluegrass Gatherin' in Webster's Chapel, Alabama, capped the evening by presenting a plaque to Charlie commemorating his induction into the Alabama Bluegrass Hall of Fame. Charlie died on January 26, 2011.

Hugh Martin

E ven people who've never heard of him are most likely familiar with his song "Have Yourself a Merry Little Christmas," one of the most cherished and often played holiday standards. Born in Birmingham on August 11, 1914, Hugh Martin was the son of parents who urged him to follow his dreams, dreams that led him to musical studies at the Birmingham Conservatory of Music at age five. Years later, while studying at Birmingham-Southern College to become a classical musician, he discovered the music of George Gershwin, conjuring new dreams that he followed straight to Broadway.

Martin moved to New York City in the 1930s to define himself over the next two decades as the vocal arranger for various Broadway shows, including Jules Styne's *Gentlemen Prefer Blondes* and *High Button Shoes* and Cole Porter's *DuBarry Was a Lady*. In 1937, he not only provided vocal arrangements but also appeared in the Broadway production of *Hooray for What?* as a singer. Soon after, he and Ralph Blane formed a vocal quartet called the Martins and appeared regularly on the Fred Allen radio show and in Irving Berlin's 1940 production of *Louisiana Purchase*, for which he and Blane also served as vocal arrangers.

Throughout the 1940s, Martin worked with Blane on a number of productions, including the Richard Rodgers and George Abbot musical *Best Foot Forward*, writing songs such as "Wish I May," "That's How I Love the Blues" and "Ev'ry Time." In 1944, they wrote songs for the now-classic film musical *Meet Me in St. Louis*, starring Judy Garland, yielding two of Martin's

Hugh Martin. *Courtesy of the Alabama Music Hall of Fame.*

most recognizable and often played songs, "Have Yourself a Merry Little Christmas" and "The Trolley Song." After collaborating with Blane to write "Love" for Lena Horne in *Ziegfeld Follies* in 1945, Martin worked on the Broadway shows *Look, Ma, I'm Dancin'* in 1948 and *Make a Wish* in 1951. He teamed with Blane again in 1955 to write "An Occasional Man" for the film *The Girl Rush*. In 1964, he collaborated with Timothy Gray to produce the Broadway musical *High Spirits*, based on Noel Coward's play *Blithe Spirits*.

Having accompanied Judy Garland on piano when she first played New York's Palace Theater and later Eddie Fisher at London's Palladium, Martin's career slowed in the late 1960s. Then, in 1979, he served as music director of the Broadway production *Sugar Babies*, starring Mickey Rooney. In 1995, he teamed with singer-pianist Michael Feinstein on the CD *Michael Feinstein Sings the Hugh Martin Songbook*. Martin, who was eighty at the time, provided gender-switched lyrics for "The Girl Next Door" and "The Trolley Song," updated lyrics to "The Two of Us" from *Look, Ma, I'm Dancin'* to refer to Feinstein and himself and played piano and sang on several of the songs.

In 2010, Martin published his autobiography, *The Boy Next Door.* Featuring a foreword by Feinstein, the book details Martin's life from his early days in Birmingham through his long and productive career. While expressing regret for having turned down *Guys and Dolls* and the inability to do *Peter Pan* due to another contract, Martin explores his life's decisions, ultimately leading to extraordinary accomplishment and recognition. But in an interview following the book's publication, Martin joked, "I don't recommend getting old. It's horrible."

In 1975, while attending the Encinitas, California Seventh-Day Adventist Church, Martin met Elaine Harrison, who became his manager and confidante. Martin credited her for changing his life and inspiring much of his church work over the last three decades of his life, reflected in his 2001 revision of his classic Christmas song to "Have Yourself a Blessed Little Christmas." He stopped playing piano in 2010, no longer satisfied with his physical ability, but continued to write without the aid of the instrument, even though he lamented that few listeners today are interested in new songs in the old style. But that's what he liked, so that's what he wrote.

Martin received several Oscar and Tony Award nominations over his long career, including a 1944 Oscar nomination for Best Original Song for "The Trolley Song" from *Meet Me in St. Louis*, 1947 Best Original Song for "Pass the Peace Pipe" from *Good News*, 1964 Tony Award Best Musical for *High Spirits* and 1990 Tony Award Best Original Score for *Meet Me in St. Louis*. In 1989, "Have Yourself a Merry Little Christmas" won ASCAP's Most Performed Feature Film Standards award. Martin was inducted into the Songwriters Hall of Fame in 1983 and Alabama Music Hall of Fame in 2001. He died at his home in California on March 11, 2011. He was ninety-six.

Jerry "Boogie" McCain

It can take decades for a musician to develop a truly personal style. Take Jerry "Boogie" McCain, for example. According to the blues harpist, he spent many years adapting and blending the styles of other harpists into something ultimately and uniquely his own. Born Paul Edward McCain in Gadsden on June 19, 1930, he was the youngest of five siblings and known, without explanation, as Jerry from birth on. With a mother who played guitar in church and a father who operated a barbecue stand that featured a Rock-Ola jukebox stocked with records of the time's best blues artists, McCain's exposure to music came early and often. By age five, Jerry had begun to play the harmonica, imitating and adapting the styles and techniques of local street musicians and the artists on his dad's jukebox such as Sonny Boy Williamson and Sonny Terry. In time, those styles melded, and his own style began to emerge as he entered his teen years.

McCain dropped out of high school in the ninth grade and began performing on local WETO radio, his upbeat delivery earning him the nickname "Boogie." But McCain soon discovered that he couldn't sustain himself on music alone— at least in the beginning—and he took other jobs that included furniture delivery, foundry work and even bounty hunter work. Throughout, he continued to develop his harp style by mimicking and parodying other harpists well enough to land him his first record deal in 1953. That year, McCain recorded "Crazy About You," a tune by the player he most admired, Little Walter Jacobs, and sent it to Lillian McMurray of Trumpet Records in Jackson, Mississippi, who subsequently invited him to record "Wine-o-Wine" and "East of the Sun."

Boogie McCain. *Photo by and courtesy of Charlie Hussey.*

McCain next recorded twelve songs for Excello in Nashville from 1955 to 1957, released only as singles at the time but defining him with distinctive lyric writing and an amplified harmonica style. McCain then returned to Gadsden and set up a recording session in his home living room, positioning the band around a single microphone to record eleven songs. The recordings weren't officially released at the time, but they appeared in 1981 as an unauthorized bootleg called *Choo Choo Rock.* Those songs and the dozen Excello recordings were released together on the 1995 CD *That's What They Want: The Best of Jerry McCain.*

Having grown up in Alabama in the early 1900s, McCain was well accustomed to segregation and discrimination, but when the civil rights movement kicked into high gear, he stood mostly on the sidelines. He strongly supported the movement's goals, but he did not actively participate for fear that he would become violent in a nonviolent cause. The only time he actively joined in the movement's activities was in 1963 when Martin Luther King spoke in Gadsden. McCain accompanied the caravan that escorted King from Birmingham to the Gadsden Galilee Baptist Church, certain that he would respond in kind if attacked. Luckily, the caravan made the trip without incident.

Musical Heritage from the Heart of Dixie

In the early days of his career, McCain played Chitlin' Circuit jukes across the South. Aware that crowds craved visual entertainment as well as music, he developed a keen ability to put on a good show, which meant more to him than his ability to play his instrument. He developed certain playing techniques that defined and endeared him to audiences, techniques that included the ability to play the harp with his nose. McCain came into his own in the 1970s and '80s, adapting a style more akin to jazz wind musicians and guitarists because he wanted to sound completely different from other blues harp players. The transition came easily because McCain is a master at improvisation and infamous for his ability to conjure tunes while performing live, an audience delight but a personal irritant because he's "lost" many of his songs due to the inability to stop the show to write them down. Some of McCain's best songs address social problems, such as the 1991 release "Burn the Crack House Down," which tackled the problem of crack cocaine use. "I don't write a song just to be writing a song to make some money," he told one interviewer. "I have to tell a story."

Over his long career, McCain married three times and fathered two daughters. He recorded with many labels, including Columbia Records

Boogie McCain's harmonica graveyard. *Photo by and courtesy of Jane DeNeefe.*

subsidiary OKeh, the most established of any. His 1962 OKeh release of Lionel Hampton's "Red Top," backed by the dance tune "Twist 62," made the *Billboard* charts, and the 1962 instrumental "Jet Stream," featuring Boots Randolph on sax, has been dubbed a classic. Since 1989, he's recorded primarily for Atlanta's Ichiban Records. In 2008, he produced the double-CD retrospective *Better Late than Never* on his own label, Boogiedown Records.

In 1996, the Etowah Youth Symphony Orchestra (EYSO) commissioned composer Julius Williams to write a work for solo harmonica and orchestra that McCain and the EYSO performed as part of Gadsden's Sesquicentennial Celebration and in June 1997 at New York City's Lincoln Center for the Performing Arts, featuring the composer conducting. In 2007, McCain received the Alabama Folk Heritage Award. He's collected a trove of paraphernalia documenting his career over the years. Calling it his "harmonica graveyard," an entire room in his home is devoted to a massive display of framed and unframed album covers, posters, tributes, plaques and old harmonicas suspended from the ceiling. Now in his eighties, McCain continues to record and perform.

Jim Nabors

S hazam!"
   "Surprise, surprise, surprise!"
   With a southern drawl and dopey expression, Jim Nabors provided catchphrases for a generation through his unforgettable, lovable portrayal of Gomer Pyle—first on the 1960s TV sitcom *The Andy Griffith Show* and then on *Gomer Pyle, USMC*—but it's Nabors's robust baritone voice that's held audiences in rapt admiration for more than five decades. The third of three children and the only boy, Nabors was born on June 12, 1930, in Sylacauga. Asthma plagued him throughout childhood but served as his inspiration to experiment with various vocal sounds, enabling him to develop the ability to control his breathing problems well enough to sing and play clarinet in his high school band. Later, majoring in business administration at UA, he got his first taste of acting, taking parts in fraternity skits.

Nabors moved to New York City after graduating college and began work as a typist at the United Nations while auditioning for acting jobs, including an unsuccessful audition for a role in Broadway's *No Time for Sergeants* in 1955. The city's air worsened his asthma, however, and he returned to Alabama to recuperate until he could take a job as assistant film editor at a Chattanooga, Tennessee TV station, where he occasionally sang on one of the locally produced daytime shows. Nabors moved to Los Angeles three years later to become a film cutter for NBC, singing nights for free at Santa Monica's Horn club to improve his vocal ability. He regularly spiced the act of arias with comical monologues about singing "opry," developing an

Jim Nabors. *Photo by John Pozadzides, courtesy of OneMansBlog.com.*

early version of the southern buffoon who would eventually endear Nabors to millions. In 1961, Bill Dana saw Nabors's act and booked him for ABC's *Steve Allen Show*. Nabors promptly quit his job at NBC, believing his singing and acting career was about to take off. He became a regular that year, but ABC cancelled future seasons of the show.

Continuing to work for free at the Horn through 1962, Nabors secured a four-month booking at the Purple Onion in San Francisco, after which he returned to Los Angeles in search of a better opportunity. It came in early 1963 when Andy Griffith saw Nabors perform at the Horn and suggested that a part in the *Andy Griffith Show* might be right for him. The resulting guest appearances as Gomer Pyle proved so popular that CBS decided to spin off a series that featured Gomer's bungling service in the U.S. Marine Corps. The series became a favorite of viewers and critics alike and one of the most popular shows on TV throughout its four-season run.

While filming the weekly sitcom, Nabors also appeared in variety specials such as *Friends and Nabors*, which proved as popular as *Gomer Pyle*, but more for his singing than Gomer's country-tinged comedy. He made numerous guest appearances on other shows as well, including the *Danny Thomas Show* and *Smothers Brothers Show*. He also performed regularly at nightclubs in Las

Vegas, Lake Tahoe and Reno and cut his first album in 1966, *Jim Nabors Sings*, which sold more than one million copies in its first year. Trying to avoid being trapped in the character that he'd so effectively created, Nabors bowed out of *Gomer Pyle, USMC* in 1969 to host the *Jim Nabors Hour*, a weekly show of comedy sketches and songs featuring a string of guest stars who included Carol Burnett, Leslie Uggams, Kate Smith, Andy Griffith, Rock Hudson and many others. One critic lauded the show for its ability to showcase Nabors's voice while retaining his "yokel status."

Throughout the early and mid-1970s, Nabors continued to guest appear on variety and talk shows, including the *Sonny and Cher Comedy Hour*, *Tonight Show* and *Dinah's Place*. In 1975, he costarred with comedian Ruth Buzzie in the sixteen-episode Saturday morning children's show *The Lost Saucer*, featuring the adventures of a time-traveling duo of androids who befriend two present-day Earth children. Nabors moved to Hawaii in 1976 but continued to accept guest roles in various TV shows and hosted a three-episode revival of the *Jim Nabors Show* in 1978. He also recorded the first in a line of albums of popular songs and Broadway show tunes while establishing several business ventures in Hawaii, including a macadamia nut and flower farm on Maui. He continued to record until 1994, when doctors discovered he had developed liver cancer, but subsequent transplant surgery proved successful.

Nabors has received many honors during his career, among them the renaming of a section of Highway 280 in Sylacauga to the Jim Nabors Highway, a star on the Hollywood Walk of Fame and the U.S. Marine Corps' official promotion of Gomer Pyle to honorary lance corporal in 2001 and to honorary corporal in 2007. He has recorded twenty-eight albums and numerous singles, hosted nightclub show runs in Hawaii, Las Vegas and Reno, acted on stage as Harold Hill in *The Music Man* and taken roles in movies such as *The Best Little Whorehouse in Texas* and *Stroker Ace*. Nabors is currently active in the operation of the Maui farm, now preserved as a park by the National Tropical Botanical Gardens. He continues to perform occasionally and travels each year, as he has since 1972, to Indianapolis, Indiana, to perform "Back Home in Indiana" at the opening of the annual Indy 500 auto race.

Sam Phillips

If it weren't for Sam Phillips, founder of the legendary Sun Records in Memphis, Tennessee, Elvis spotting would never have become a sport. Phillips had an innate ability for discovering talent bound for superstardom, talent that included Elvis, Johnny Cash, B.B. King, Jerry Lee Lewis and Carl Perkins. And because of Phillips's ability, he became one of the most important music producers in American history.

Born in Florence on January 5, 1923, Phillips was the youngest of his family's eight children, growing up in Depression-era Alabama, listening to gospel music, country music and blues sung by fieldworkers and street performers. As a teen, he joined the Coffee High School band, playing sousaphone, trombone and drums, and eventually conducted the band. When his father died in 1941, he dropped out of school shortly before graduation to support his mother and aunt. He married Rebecca Burns in 1942 (they later had two children, Knox and Jerry) and considered studying law, but music proved his passion, leading him to take an extension course in audio engineering from Alabama Polytechnic Institution and then a job at a Muscle Shoals radio station, where he hosted a religious program.

From 1942 through 1949, Phillips worked at several radio stations in Alabama and southern Tennessee before taking a position at WREC in Memphis. He learned a lot about recording and record production at the stations and was keenly aware of how local musicians had to travel to Chicago, Nashville and New Orleans to record. In 1950, he opened Memphis Recording Service, a small studio at 706 Union Avenue, where he

Sam Phillips at Sun Studio. *Courtesy of the Alabama Music Hall of Fame.*

provided cheap recording services for musicians and mobile recordings for private events such as weddings. But he wanted to do more. He wanted to make a difference.

Phillips initially relied on established labels to produce and distribute his studio's recordings, but disputes arose, leading him to start Phillips Records. The label's first release, Joe Hill Louis's "Boogie in the Park," attracted attention from B.B. King, Howlin' Wolf and Ike Turner, but the label folded only for Phillips to start Sun Records in 1952. Jackie Brenston and the Delta Cats' "Rocket 88" with Ike Turner on guitar became Sun's first hit, going to number one on the R&B charts. Phillips quit his job at WREC to produce full time and released Johnny London's "Drivin' Slow," followed by Rufus Thomas's "Bear Cat," a big hit for the company but one found by a jury to have plagiarized the Big Mama Thornton version of "Hound Dog," forcing Sun to give up a large percentage of the record's royalties. Sun continued to produce moderately successful blues records and white country musicians over the next couple of years, with Phillips taking chances other producers

Sam Phillips and
Elvis Presley. *Courtesy
of the Alabama Music
Hall of Fame.*

wouldn't, recording distorted guitars and harmonicas at high levels on songs
that others would have toned down or discarded altogether. Then, in 1954,
gold walked in.

Recording two songs as a birthday gift for his mother, Elvis Presley impressed
Phillips enough to invite the young man back in July to make a record for
the company. That record was "That's Alright (Mama)." Phillips signed
Elvis, made five records, ten songs in all, and delivered them to prominent
stations throughout the South while booking Elvis in performances across
the country. In 1954, Phillips sold Elvis's contract to RCA for $35,000, later
calling it the worst business decision he'd ever made. Nevertheless, the deal
enabled Phillips to expand Sun and develop other young artists, including
Jerry Lee Lewis, Johnny Cash, Carl Perkins and Roy Orbison. Perkins's
"Blue Suede Shoes" gave the company its first national hit.

While concentrating on rockabilly throughout the 1950s, Phillips proved
to be a gifted producer, unafraid to experiment, resulting in a distinguishable
"Sun sound." But as the 1950s ended, interest in rockabilly waned, and

Phillips couldn't sustain Sun's previous success. In 1961, he moved the studio into a larger building on Madison Avenue in Memphis to increase the diversity and output of the company's music. Perkins, Orbison and Cash went to other labels, however, and Sun lost its momentum despite a few hits by Charlie Rich and attempts by Jerry Lee Lewis. Meanwhile, Phillips invested in real estate properties and the Holiday Inn hotel chain and purchased several radio stations. In 1969, he retired from the music business and sold the Sun Records catalogue to Shelby Singleton. Reissues continue through the present day, and Sun Studio remains open to musicians and tourists. An inductee of the Rock and Roll Hall of Fame, Alabama Music Hall of Fame, Country Music Hall of Fame and Rockabilly Hall of Fame, Phillips died of respiratory failure on August 1, 2003, and is buried at Memphis's Memorial Park.

Wilson Pickett

With "Mustang Sally" and "In the Midnight Hour" on *Rolling Stone*'s five hundred all-time greatest songs list, Pratt native Wilson Pickett ranks as one of the most successful R&B artists of the twentieth century. Born on March 18, 1941, Pickett was the youngest of eleven children who grew up picking cotton under the guidance of a grandfather who tolerated none of the day's "devil's music." Perhaps it was the hard work and demanding grandfather, but whatever the reason, Pickett developed a strong defiance and self-confidence he displayed with everyone, including whites and especially the field boss. On Sundays, he would sing in his local church, but his determination to be himself and his defiance toward authority eventually netted him the nickname the "Wicked Pickett" and numerous beatings from his grandfather and mother determined to force the wickedness out of him.

After his parents divorced, Pickett fled Alabama in 1955 to live with his father in Detroit, Michigan, where his singing career began in earnest when he joined the Violinaires gospel quartet. He distinguished himself by using a method he'd learned back in Alabama called the "moan," a technique common to early African American spirituals and later incorporated into gospel and R&B music. Despite the Violinaires' success, Pickett's "wicked" desires for the "devil's" music surfaced, and he soon left the quartet to join the Falcons R&B group. The Falcons also featured Mack Rice and Eddie Floyd and were noted for blending R&B with gospel and blues in songs such as "I Found a Love."

Although the featured lead on several songs, Pickett left the group in 1963 to pursue a solo career. He signed with Double L Records, which later sold

Wilson Pickett and Jerry Wexler at FAME. *Courtesy of the Alabama Music Hall of Fame.*

his contract to Atlantic, where he began work with producer Jerry Wexler. Wexler first took Pickett to Memphis's Stax Records to record several singles, including "In the Midnight Hour" and "634-5789," which established the singer as a crossover artist. In 1966, Pickett returned to Alabama as a result of Wexler's newly established relationship with Rick Hall and FAME Studios in Muscle Shoals. Pickett was at first skeptical that a white producer and backing musicians could deliver the sound and soul he demanded. But then recording got underway, and Pickett was delighted with results that included the hits "Land of a Thousand Dances" and "Mustang Sally."

In 1970, Pickett recorded at Philadelphia's Sigma Sound, producing two of his biggest hits, "Engine Number Nine" and "Don't Let the Green Grass Fool You," which featured the lavish orchestration that defined the "Philadelphia sound." Although he later recorded a few more charting songs at Muscle Shoals, Pickett's star began to fade in the early 1970s. As he continued to tour, he continued to portray himself as the defiant, self-confident man of his youth even as personal problems began to mount. Following several drug convictions, he was arrested in 1991 for yelling death threats as he drove a car over the Englewood, New Jersey mayor's lawn. In 1992, police charged him for assaulting his girlfriend. In 1993, the car he was driving struck an eighty-six-year-old pedestrian who later died. Pickett pled guilty to charges of drunken driving and was sentenced to a year in jail and five years' probation.

Despite his personal problems, Pickett pressed on with his career. Following the 1991 movie *The Commitments*, which centers on an Irish R&B band desperate to meet Pickett, he released *It's Harder Now* as his comeback album. Although critically acclaimed, the album proved a commercial flop. Pickett continued to perform into the twenty-first century and was featured in the 2002 documentary *Only the Strong Survive*, but health problems began to take a toll, and he was hospitalized several times throughout 2005. On January 19, 2006, in Ashburn, Virginia, he died of a heart attack, leaving behind his partner, Gail Webb, two sons and two daughters. Little Richard delivered the eulogy at Pickett's memorial service, reminding the crowd that Pickett's passion and raspy voice had opened new avenues in music, preparing the way for artists such as Sean "P. Diddy" Combs and Marshall Bruce Mathers III, known as Eminem.

Many of Pickett's songs remain radio staples and are covered by scores of performers. He received numerous awards during his career, including induction into the Rock and Roll Hall of Fame in 1991, the Pioneer Award from the Rhythm and Blues Foundation in 1993 and induction into the Alabama Music Hall of Fame in 1999. Pickett was one of the primary artists who incorporated an aggressive style and sound into soul music, a style that defined his personal performances.

Martha Reeves

Called "earthier" and "more aggressive" than other female groups, Martha Reeves and the Vandellas became one of the most popular "girl acts" of the 1960s. In 1961, William Stevenson, Motown's artist and repertoire director, described Reeves's voice as "the sound of young America," a sound that got the singer an invitation to audition at the new Motown Records Detroit headquarters, "Hitsville, USA," but the audition never materialized, setting the young singer on a path that would lead to the Vandellas and beyond.

Born in Eufala on July 18, 1941, Reeves—one of eleven children—grew up in Detroit, developing an early love for music, spending most of her childhood singing in her grandfather's church and taking voice lessons in high school from Abraham Silver, who coached other notable singers such as the Supremes' Florence Ballard and Mary Wilson and the Miracles' Bobby Rogers. After graduating high school, she began singing professionally in 1959 when she joined the Fascinations. The following year, she cofounded the Del-Phis, from which the Vandellas later emerged, performing at local talent shows and backing without credit Mike Hanks on his record "The Hawk" and Leon Peterson on "I Know You Know." Their first credited backing was on J.J. Barnes's 1962 release "Won't You Let Me Know." And though their work led to recording "My Baby Won't Come Back" for Chess-Mate Records in 1961, the song failed to chart.

Reeves won a local contest that same year, the prize being a three-day engagement at the Twenty Grand nightclub, where she billed herself

Martha Reeves. *Courtesy of Martha Reeves.*

as Martha LaVaille and where Stevenson heard her perform, leading to his invitation to audition for Motown. Although the audition failed to materialize, Stevenson hired her as his personal secretary, which provided her with an intimate education in recording business operations. In 1962, her chance to record came when Motown head Berry Gordy needed singers for a session with Marvin Gaye. He recruited Reeves and the other Del-Phis members Gloria Williamson, Annette Beard and Rosalind Ashford to back Gaye on what would be his first hit, "Stubborn Kind of Fellow." A month later, Reeves filled in for Mary Wells on a recording session, impressing Stevenson enough to record the Del-Phis performing "You'll Never Cherish a Love So True ('Til You Lose It)." At that point, Williamson dropped out of the group, unwilling to leave her job to sing full time. Reeves—now lead vocalist—and the remaining members renamed the group Martha and the Vandellas, deriving the name from Martha's favorite singer, Della Reese.

Over the next few years, the trio charted numerous hits, including "Heat Wave" and "Jimmy Mack." By 1973, the group disbanded after going through several member changes. Meanwhile, Motown transferred its offices from Detroit to Los Angeles, but Reeves refused to go, instead suing for and winning release from her contract. She then signed with MCA to cut the album *Martha Reeves*, a mix of pop, rock and R&B covers, but the album did not sell well. In 1977, she signed with Arista to produce *The Rest of My Life*, but it, too, failed commercially. After moving to Fantasy in 1978, she released *We Meet Again*. In the early 1980s, she worked on various Motown package tours with a new version of the Vandellas. Then, in 1989, she reunited with original members Sterling and Holmes to cut the single "Step into My Shoes" for British producer Ian Levine's Motor City label. In 1996, she headlined the national touring version of the musical *Ain't Misbehaving* and later toured for three years in the United Kingdom in the musical revue *Dancing in the Streets*.

Then came the economic downturn of the 2000s, hitting Detroit particularly hard, and Reeves felt compelled to enter politics as a way to help the city she loved. Detroit residents elected her as a city councilor in 2004, based on her promise to inspire the city's diverse cultures and communities to work together in resurrecting the city's economy. Reeves served four years on the council before returning to music full time. Since then, she has been featured in the PBS special *Motown: The Early Years* and has released several CDs, including *Spellbound: Motown Lost & Found (1962 1972)* and *The Definitive Collection*.

Reeves has received numerous awards over the years, including the Dinah Washington Award and induction into the Alabama Music Hall of Fame, Rock and Roll Hall of Fame and Vocal Group Hall of Fame. As she approached her seventieth birthday in 2011, she continued to perform around the world and work as an advocate for Detroit schools and seniors.

Clarence "Pinetop" Smith and Charles Edward "Cow Cow" Davenport

Boogie-woogie—that fast-paced, upbeat style of piano blues, with its prominent walking bass and treble line variations—may owe its initial popularity to pianists Jimmy Yancey, Albert Ammons and Clarence "Pinetop" Smith, but it's Pinetop Smith who gave the style its name. Born on June 11, 1904, in Troy and growing up in Birmingham, Smith earned the nickname "Pinetop" purportedly because of his love of climbing tall trees. He must have preferred his perch before the piano even more, as he taught himself to play, transforming the blues structure into a new genre, a faster, purely instrumental piano form played primarily for dancing in African American barrelhouses throughout the South during the early 1900s.

In 1920, Smith moved to Pittsburgh, Pennsylvania, where he began work on the Theater Owners Booking Association (TOBA) vaudeville circuit as a comedian, pianist and singer, backing blues vocalist Ma Rainey for a while. In the late 1920s, he met Charles Edward "Cow Cow" Davenport on the circuit. Born in Anniston on April 23, 1894, Davenport learned to play piano from his mother, but the family thought he would take up preaching like his father until a fateful night in 1911 when he was expelled from Alabama Theological Seminary for playing ragtime at a church function. He went to work as a medicine show musician, developing his ragtime piano style and moving into vaudeville with blues singer Dora Carr to perform as Davenport and Company. The two made a few recordings in 1925 and 1926 but broke up shortly after Carr married. By then, Davenport had become one of the most distinctive and copied boogie-woogie stylists of the time, even though the term boogie-woogie hadn't yet been coined.

Besides performing, Davenport was working as a talent scout for Vocalion records and recommended Smith to the company. In 1928, Smith moved with his wife and young son to Chicago, where he recorded "Pinetop's Boogie-Woogie" (sometimes credited as "Pine Top's Boogie-Woogie") in December, one of the first songs of the genre to become a hit and *the* song that gave the genre its name. Until then, no one had used the term "boogie-woogie," at least in a song title. Smith, talking over the music on the record, directs listeners how to "boogie-woogie," "mess around" and "shake that thing," catchphrases that remain popular today. Smith booked his next recording session for March, but he died from a gunshot wound during a Chicago dance hall fight the day before the session.

Over the years, various stories circulated about his death, many without any basis. In one story, Smith had supposedly written "Pinetop's Boogie-Woogie" for Bessie Rose, who lived in Galveston, Texas, although he had gone on record that he'd written it during a rent party in St. Louis, Missouri. In the Texas story, he was playing Galveston's Naked Club, and though he usually reserved the boogie for Rose, he decided to sing it to another woman. When Rose came in, she drew a knife and buried the blade in Smith's back. To lay such myths to rest, *Down Beat* ran Smith's death certificate facts in 1939, detailing that Smith had died from a stray pistol bullet in a Chicago dance hall when two men got into a scuffle and a third man ran toward them with a pistol that discharged. Smith was twenty-four when he died, leaving behind his wife and two young children, having recorded fewer than a dozen tracks. No photographs of Smith are known to exist.

Moving to Cleveland, Ohio, in 1930, Davenport recorded with Sam Price and began touring again on the TOBA circuit. In 1938, a stroke paralyzed his right hand, but he continued to work as a vocalist and eventually regained strength in his hand enough to play again. In the early 1940s, he stopped touring and took a job as a washroom attendant at New York's Onyx Club. When Freddie Slack's Orchestra hit with Davenport's "Cow Cow Boogie," sparking the boogie-woogie craze of the 1940s, Davenport returned to recording on the Comet and Circle labels. Recurring sickness, however, prevented him from making a full comeback, and he died in 1955 in Cleveland from heart problems. He's best remembered for "(I'll Be Glad When You're Dead) You Rascal You" and "Cow Cow Boogie."

The Stripling Brothers

Most acts in the early twentieth century—country or otherwise—didn't get rich off their music. Receiving more than token payment for their records was considered lucky. The difference between those who made it and those who didn't rested on two things: talent and determination. Charlie and Ira Stripling, born in Pickens County on August 8, 1896, and June 5, 1898, respectively, had six siblings and learned young the value of dedication, developing a keen taste for music early on. Charlie acquired a fiddle and learned his first songs from Pleasant C. Carroll, a neighbor known as Uncle Plez. Ira bought a six-dollar mail-order guitar and developed a strong playing style to complement Charlie's fiddling, and they began to compete in area fiddlers' conventions. Although the events offered little in the way of money, money became an important goal for Charlie at age twenty-two when he married fourteen-year-old Tellie Sullivan. In their years together, they had six children, which proved a strain on the tenant farmer's budget. The potential extra income from music contests, no matter how slight, pushed Charlie to develop his skills to a level that few could match.

In 1923, Atlanta's Fiddling John Carson recorded an old-time fiddling tune that became a hit, especially among rural listeners. Record companies quickly realized the potential of rural audiences and set up temporary studios in cities throughout the South in search of fiddlers, shape-note singers, gospel groups and string bands. When the Brunswick-Balke-Collender Company came to Bankhead Hotel in Birmingham, the brothers recorded two songs in hopes of landing a contract. While in Birmingham, they also appeared on WAPI radio,

The Stripling Brothers. *Courtesy of the Stripling Family Archives.*

resulting in numerous dance bookings in north Alabama mining towns where they received endless audience requests for "foxtrots" and "toddles." The Striplings thus created what they called "ragtime breakdowns," danceable syncopated tunes based on popular music of the day.

When Brunswick failed to contact the brothers in the weeks after the recording session, the Striplings assumed the songs had not been published, but ten months later, Charlie heard one of their songs playing on a record in a store in Fayette. When he contacted the Brunswick Company in Chicago, Jack Kapp, the man who'd supervised the Birmingham recording, told the brothers he was surprised they had not been paid, and he immediately invited them to Chicago to record at least a dozen more selections, promising to pay them when they came. The brothers balked, suspicious that they'd be stiffed, and said they'd come only if the company paid their expenses in advance. The company wired them the money, and they left the following day. After recording for Brunswick, the brothers began recording in New York for Decca in 1934, but tragedy struck in the form of Tellie's death, leaving Charlie with six children under the age of fifteen. He later married Myrtle Wheeler and fathered three more children.

Decca had given the brothers a choice of a fifty-dollars-per-record flat fee or a one-cent-per-record royalty. They chose the flat fee and relied heavily on income from performing, Charlie's sharecropping and Ira's income from the store he owned and operated in Alabama. In the final session for Decca in 1936, they recorded their last fourteen songs as a duo. Ira then returned home to run his store full time, unable to continue to pay an employee to operate it while he was away.

Charlie then formed a group with his sons Robert Clifton and Lee Edwin, born in 1920 and 1921, respectively. When the boys entered military service in World War II, Charlie formed another band and continued to play through the 1950s. At age sixty, his career ended when he suffered severe stomach pain during a concert and was hospitalized for an extended period. With the onset of arthritis, he lost his ability to play. He died on January 19, 1966, and is buried in Mount Zion Primitive Baptist Church cemetery near his birthplace, the same cemetery in which Uncle Plez (1850–1930) is buried. Ira died a year later on March 11, 1967, and is also buried in Mount Zion cemetery.

During their career, Charlie and Ira recorded forty-two songs as the Stripling Brothers. In 1971, County Records reissued thirteen of the recordings, exposing new generations to their music. As a result, Charlie Stripling is now regarded as one of the most important and influential old-time American fiddlers.

Charlie's son Robert became a minister, and Lee settled in Seattle. After the reissue of the original Stripling Brothers' songs, musicians began stopping by Lee's home to hear "authentic" fiddle music played live. In 2000, Lee began to perform again at dances, retirement homes, cafés and music festivals. In November 2010, Seattle filmmaker Jeri Vaughn's *Winging My Way Back Home: The Stripling Fiddle Legacy*, a documentary on the brothers, their father and uncle and their music, premiered at the Charlie Stripling Fiddlefest and Fish Fry in Belk, Alabama, shortly after the deaths of both Lee and Robert. Lee died from lung cancer on April 20, 2009, and Robert died in his sleep at home in Montgomery on October 26, 2010.

Sun Ra

"In tomorrow's world," he insisted in 1956, "men will not need artificial instruments such as jets and spaceships. In the world of tomorrow, the new man will *think* the place he wants to go, then his mind will take him there." Eventually shrouding his past in mystery and taking the name of an Egyptian god, Herman "Sonny" Blount was born in Birmingham on May 22, 1914, and no matter where he would later claim to have originated, he brought to the world some of the most innovative jazz of the time, leading the genre in new directions that continue to influence artists today.

Under the direction of John "Fess" Whatley, Blount displayed considerable talent while playing in Birmingham Industrial High School bands and at social functions. Graduating in 1932, Blount became infatuated with jazz and began an extensive collection of jazz recordings, transcribing and practicing tunes that he liked most, especially several by Fletcher Henderson, including "King Porter Stomp" and "Queer Notions." By 1934, Blount had begun touring in a band led by Ethel Harper, a biology teacher who wanted to be a singer so much that she left Blount in charge of her band in mid-tour to join an all-vocal group. The following year, Blount entered Alabama A&M University on a scholarship from Dr. S.F. Harris, who provided educational help for several musicians from Blount's high school.

With plans to major in music education, Blount received considerable classical training in college, ending his first year with a grade point average of 3.18, ranking eighth in his class. But something happened that year. In one account, he had a transformative dream. In another, he traveled through

Sun Ra. *Photo by and courtesy of Ian Lawton.*

a beam of light to Saturn, where aliens warned him of impending chaos on Earth, a time when the world would listen to him when he spoke. Whatever the reason or inspiration, he left the university at the end of the year to return to Birmingham and lead the Sonny Blount Orchestra, making it into one of the most respected swing bands in Alabama, one that played exclusively to black audiences. He also developed a keen ability to arrange and transpose music from key to key to make it more accessible for different instruments.

In 1942, he was drafted into military service, but he refused to go, claiming conscientious objector status. Unable to substantiate the claim, the government jailed him at a Pennsylvania civilian public service camp, where he claimed to suffer from physical burning and aching. In March 1943, he was released due to poor health, a condition that miraculously cleared when he received 4F status.

In 1946, he moved to Chicago, where he worked for a short time with bandleader Fletcher Henderson and then saxophonist Coleman Hawkins before playing for dancers and floor shows while wearing exotic costumes. Recording bands to later transcribe their arrangements, Blount advocated anything musically innovative and added electric instruments to his band as soon as they became available. Interest and belief in Egypt and the mysteries of space as a means to empower the black community also deepened, and on October 22, 1952, he discarded the name Sonny Blount for the name Le Sony'r Ra, based on the name of the Egyptian sun god Ra. He then took his band, the Arkestra (derived by combining "orchestra" and "Ark," referring to the Ark of the Covenant), in avant-garde directions, encouraging the musicians to "play with the warmth of the sun…all the things you don't know" because "there's an infinity of what you don't know."

Known by several names, including Solar Myth Arkestra and Astro-Intergalactic Infinity Arkestra, the band became a part of Sun Ra's mythical world and a component of his performance art. In the early years, the Arkestra reflected big band influences, but Sun Ra insisted on improvisation and experimentation, forcing members fully into modern avant-garde sounds, shunning predictable rhythm patterns common to popular music. Performing in long, rich robes, Arkestra members incorporated elements of science fiction, Afrocentrism and Egyptology into performances, while Sun Ra appeared in elaborate, Egyptian-inspired headdresses that displayed cosmic scenes. Extravagant light displays and dancers accompanied performances as well.

Sun Ra moved the Arkestra to New York in the early 1960s and then settled in Philadelphia in 1968, influencing both jazz and rock by then, including bands like Sonic Youth and Pink Floyd. Taking a break from constant touring in 1971, the Arkestra stayed with the Black Panthers' Bobby Seale in Oakland at Seale's invitation, and Sun Ra taught a class entitled "The Black Man in the Cosmos" at the University of California–Berkeley.

Sun Ra demanded a lot from himself and his band members, banning drugs, alcohol and fraternization with women and taking a personal vow of celibacy when he changed his name, never marrying or fathering any children. After the pause in 1971, the Arkestra maintained a heavy touring schedule until the early 1990s, when Sun Ra's health declined drastically. He returned to Birmingham in 1993 to be with relatives and died on May 30 from pneumonia. He is buried in Elmwood Cemetery.

Sun Ra ranks as one of history's most inventive jazz musicians and certainly one of the most flamboyant. Decades before the indie music movement, he released more than one hundred self-produced albums on his own Saturn label and distributed them at concerts and through a few select record stores. The subject of several films and books, Sun Ra was inducted into the Alabama Jazz Hall of Fame in 1979. Sun Ra's Arkestra continues to perform under the direction of saxophonist Marshall Allen, who joined the Arkestra in 1958.

Ward Swingle

Ward Swingle's music is quite different from what most people expect to hear from an Alabama native. It is music that defies class and genre to capture and delight a worldwide audience through innovation and sheer celebration of sound. Born in Mobile on September 21, 1927, Ward Swingle's childhood musical education was uncommon for most in Alabama, immersed in jazz influences from nearby New Orleans. As a teenager, Swingle played in area big bands, experience that served him well when he entered Cincinnati Conservatory, where he later graduated summa cum laude. His musical hunger next led him to study with pianist Walter Gieseking in postwar France, where, in the 1960s, he established an extraordinarily innovative group of singers who changed the way the world listens to music by Johann Sebastian Bach.

It began in 1959 in Paris when Swingle and Mimi Perrin formed the six-member vocal jazz group Les Double Six of Paris, utilizing overdubbing to render twelve-part singing to interpret jazz songs in the French jazz standard, with improvisational vocals imitating various instruments. By the time it disbanded in 1965, the group had recorded four albums.

While singing with Les Double Six, Swingle contemplated the treatment of Bach compositions in the same manner as jazz songs. He pitched the idea in 1963 to seven Paris freelance session singers bored with pop and rock, and they agreed that it sounded intriguing. He then chose pieces from Bach's *Well Tempered Clavier*, each of its two volumes containing a prelude and fugue in the chromatic scale's major and minor keys. Retaining every

Ward Swingle (fourth from left, seated row) and the original Swingle Singers. *Courtesy of Ward Swingle.*

original note, Swingle adapted the pieces for vocal rendering while also adding a rhythm section. Calling themselves the Swingle Singers, the group then convinced Philips Records to record an album as a Christmas present for family and friends, but it became much, much more when it was released in 1963 as *Bach's Greatest Hits*. The album ultimately charted in the Top 10 and remained in the Top 100 for nearly two years. *Bach's Greatest Hits* and the two albums that followed—*Going Baroque* and *Anyone for Mozart?*—earned the group a Grammy for Best Performance by a Chorus, while *Bach's Greatest Hits* also won the Best New Artist Grammy. The group won another Best Choral Performance Grammy in 1969 for *Berio: Sinfonia*.

Unlike Double Six, the Swingle Singers did not overdub recordings, so performing recorded pieces live was a comparatively easy task, and the group found eager audiences worldwide. Swingle remained close to Bach's written scores in all vocal arrangements, adding drums and bass to accentuate a piece's rhythm while developing an exciting new style that utilized singers' voices as instruments to meld jazz and classical elements into delightful feasts of sound. As popularity grew, the group attracted the attention of several composers whose works proved particularly adaptable, including avant-

Ward Swingle. *Courtesy of Ward Swingle.*

garde composer Luciano Berio's *Sinfonia* for orchestra and eight voices, which the group performed in 1969 with the New York Philharmonic. Other contributing composers included John Dankworth, Pascal Zavaro, Azio Corghi and Michael Nyman.

By 1973, the Swingle Singers had recorded thirteen albums. Swingle then left the group to move to Great Britain, where he formed a new group under the same name, expanding the repertoire to include English choral traditions. Swingle continued performing with that group until 1985, when he returned to the United States to lecture and guest conduct for the next decade while remaining musical adviser to subsequent incarnations of the Swingle Singers, always refining the style and expanding the repertoire.

Throughout the group's history, Swingle has provided the singers with new challenges to maintain interest by expanding the repertoire. Examples include the arrangement of the "Overture to the Marriage of Figaro" for eight voices, which the group has used to open many concerts. One of the more astonishing crowd-pleasers is often saved for encores—"Flight of the Bumble Bee," sung as fast as possible, using a variety of scat syllables that lend themselves to speed.

Swingle returned in 1994 to France, where he continues to arrange, compose, guest conduct and advise the current Swingle Singers group.

His book, *Swingle Singing*, recounting his career and explaining the Swingle singing method with illustrations from his arrangements, was published in the mid-1990s. In 2004, the French minister of culture and information named Swingle *officier de l'Ordre des Arts des Lettres* (officer of the Order of Arts and Letters).

In 2007, documentary filmmaker Michael Lawrence interviewed a wide range of composers and musicians as he explored the work and life of Johann Sebastian Bach for *Bach & Friends*, a documentary complete with performances by those interviewed. One section features Swingle recounting the Swingle Singers' origin and footage of Swingle conducting the group. Now based in London, England, the Swingle Singers continue to perform a variety of shows each year, from a cappella to orchestral and contemporary light opera, consistently adding to the repertoire and refining the group's unique and enduring style.

Toni Tennille, Jim Mahaffey and Dave Edwards

Auburn University's big band, the Auburn Knights, has been performing professionally since September 1930, with graduates going on to play with such greats as Count Basie, Tommy Dorsey, Lawrence Welk and many others. While the flow of Knights musicians into such professional bands has been impressive, the 1959–60 incarnation is particularly notable for setting three extremely talented performers on diverse musical career paths.

In the 1970s, former Auburn Knights singer Toni Tennille composed half of one of the most successful acts in popular music. Born on May 8, 1940, in Montgomery, Cathryn Antoinette "Toni" Tennille has always had music in her life. Her father, Frank, sang with the first Auburn Knights and later under the stage name Clark Randall with Bob Crosby and the Bobcats. Tennille's own music career began with classical piano studies as a child and singing with the Auburn Knights in college in 1959 and 1960.

Besides Tennille, the 1959–60 Knights featured two other musicians who would have honored careers in music. Born on January 24, 1939, Montevallo native Jim Mahaffey played lead trumpet for the Knights. After graduating, he taught band for thirty-two years, ranging from elementary to university and graduate-level courses, music theory, trumpet, arranging and jazz ensemble, but his national fame is rooted in his arrangements and compositions, with more than 125 publications to his credit. As a musician, he's played lead trumpet for Warren Covington, Billy Butterfield, June Christy, Fred Waring's "Kid From Home" and the Tommy Dorsey Orchestra.

The Auburn Knights, featuring Toni Tennille (front row, far right), Jim Mahaffey (back row, third from left) and Dave Edwards (front row, second from left). *Courtesy of Jim Mahaffey.*

Sax player David W. "Dave" Edwards also launched his music career with the 1959–60 Auburn Knights. Born in Opelika on January 11, 1941, Edwards specialized in the big band style, playing flute, saxophone and clarinet. After leaving Auburn, Edwards performed with the Glenn Miller Orchestra and Richard Malty before entering the army, where he played with the NORAD Commanders Jazz Band for the duration of his service. In 1968, he joined the Lawrence Welk Orchestra, occupying the reed section's first chair and becoming a familiar face on Welk's weekly television show.

With her father singing and her mother hosting a Montgomery daytime TV talk show, Tennille became well acquainted with public performance. By 1971, she was in San Francisco, performing in an original musical entitled *Mother Earth*. She met her future husband and musical partner, Daryl Dragon, after he attended a performance. On a break from touring with the Beach Boys, who had dubbed him "The Captain" because he often wore a skipper's hat, Dragon invited Tennille to join him on keyboards with the band when they resumed touring. She became the first and last female Beach Boys member.

After the tour, Tennille and Dragon performed as a duo in the San Fernando Valley area, where she also did studio work, including backing vocals for cuts on Pink Floyd's *The Wall* and Elton John's "Don't Let the Sun Go Down on Me." When two local disc jockeys promised airplay, she and Dragon recorded Tennille's "The Way I Want to Touch You." The song became a regional hit, attracting the attention of several record labels, and they eventually signed with A&M. The duo made their first album a family affair, bringing in Tennille's three sisters for backing vocals and one of Dragon's brothers to engineer and play drums on several of the songs. In 1975, "Love Will Keep Us Together" became their first national hit. The couple married that November and followed the hit with the national release of "The Way I Want to Touch You," which rose to number four.

During their career, the duo recorded nine albums and had fourteen hit singles, including "Muskrat Love," a song that Dragon thought rather silly although it proved to be one of the duo's most beloved. From 1975 through 1980, the duo hosted TV's *The Captain & Tennille Variety Show* and three specials in later years. Tennille also hosted the syndicated *Toni Tennille Variety Talk Show* in 1980.

As the duo's popularity waned in the early 1980s, Tennille began performing jazz and pop standards with U.S. and Canadian orchestras, recording several albums of standards, including *Incurably Romantic*, *More than You Know*, *All of Me* and *Tennille Sings Big Band*, all garnering favorable critical response. In 1998 and 1999, she starred in the national tour of the musical *Victor/Victoria*, playing the Victoria Grant character as an "Alabama contralto" to critical praise. The original version's references to England were changed to places in Alabama and the South for Tennille's version.

The Auburn Knights continue to perform seven decades after inception, featuring dedicated student musicians, many continuing in music professions after graduation. In 2007, Tennille and Dragon settled in Prescott, Arizona, where Tennille continues to perform occasionally. Diagnosed with Parkinson's disease, Dragon does little to no public performing but still practices privately and maintains the couple's websites. Mahaffey has retired from teaching and now resides in San Antonio, Texas, where he continues to arrange and compose through Southern Music Company. His works are featured on the CDs *New Horizons: Concert Music of Jim Mahaffey*, *Live at the Radius: The Music of Jim Mahaffey* and *Primetime*. Edwards left the Lawrence Welk Orchestra in 1979 to pursue a solo career, which eventually led him to Florida, where he worked with local and nationally touring bands. His career ended tragically when he suffered a fatal heart attack on August 12, 2000.

Willie Mae "Big Mama" Thornton

A formidable woman who liked to wear men's clothing, Willie Mae "Big Mama" Thornton belted out songs well enough to be grouped with Ma Rainey and Bessie Smith as one of the best blues singers ever. Born on December 11, 1926, the Montgomery native began singing as a child in her dad's church choir and quit school as a teen when her mother died, taking a job cleaning a bar to earn extra money to help support her dad and six other siblings. Having taught herself to play drums and harmonica, Big Mama began her blues career unexpectedly one night when the bar's scheduled singer didn't show. Her break into national performance later came when promoter Sammy Green heard her sing—either at the bar or when she won a local contest, depending on the source—which led to him signing her in 1941 to tour with his Atlanta-based Hot Harlem Review, a gig that lasted seven years.

In 1948, Thornton relocated to Houston to work the club scene. There, she contributed to the development of the "Texas blues" style before meeting Peacock Records owner Don Robey, who signed her to a five-year contract. By 1952, she was pushing three hundred pounds when she began touring with the Johnny Otis Rhythm and Blues Caravan, her masculine voice proving a massive presence and audience favorite. Then, in 1953, her biggest hit came with Jerry Lieber and Mike Stoller's "Hound Dog," reaching number one on *Billboard*'s R&B chart, selling more than a half-million copies. For her effort, though, Thornton earned a mere $500 flat fee and no royalties, even on later-year reissues. Three years after Thornton's version and with revised,

Big Mama
Thornton. *Courtesy
of Hohner, Inc.*

less sensual lyrics, Elvis Presley hit number one with a mainstream version. Thornton would end live performances of the song in later years with "bow wow to you, too," a jab at Elvis's success with the song she first made famous.

Despite Thornton's preference for men's clothing, early promoters insisted she wear dresses onstage, but she asserted herself over the years. By the end of her career, she was performing in a man's suit jacket and straw hat. Rumors circulated off and on about lesbian affairs, but little to no evidence exists to support or debunk the claims.

Like many performers, tragedy marked her life. Some sources claim that she gave birth to a son who was removed from her custody by state authorities before she left Alabama. In 1954, she suffered a shocking personal loss when her friend, singer Johnny Ace, killed himself minutes before their scheduled Christmas Eve show in Houston, Texas. With his girlfriend in his lap, Ace had been joking and waving a pistol around. When he put the barrel to his girlfriend's head, Thornton shouted for him to stop before he killed someone.

He laughed, said the gun had only one bullet in it and that he knew exactly where it was. He raised the gun to his temple and pulled the trigger.

As R&B's popularity began to wane in the late 1950s, Thornton moved to San Francisco when her agreement with Peacock Records expired. She performed regularly with Clarence "Gatemouth" Brown and got another shot at widespread success in 1960 when she wrote and recorded "Ball & Chain." But the record company held copyright in its name, not Thornton's, denying Thornton royalty income from sales when Janis Joplin's cover became a hit. Joplin, however, promoted Thornton as the song's author, and Thornton enjoyed renewed popularity during the traditional blues revival in the mid-1960s. She became a regular at the Monterey Jazz Festival and toured Europe with the American Folk Blues Festival in 1965.

In the late 1960s, Arhoolie Records signed Thornton to record several albums, including *Big Mama Thornton: In Europe, Big Mama Thornton with the Chicago Blues Band* and *Ball & Chain*. With Joplin using "Ball & Chain" as her signature song, Thornton's popularity continued to grow, leading to her appearance at the Sky River Rock Festival in 1968, which featured such artists as Country Joe and the Fish, Richard Pryor, It's a Beautiful Day, the Youngbloods, New Lost City Ramblers and the Grateful Dead.

A heavy drinker throughout her life, Thornton continued to perform into the 1970s even as her health declined, recording the albums *Saved, She's Back, Jail* and *Sassy Mama!* In 1983, despite requiring onstage assistance as she recovered from serious injuries received in a car accident, Thornton performed at the Newport Jazz Festival with Eddie Vinson, B.B. King and Muddy Waters, giving what critics called the performance of a lifetime and resulting in a Buddha Records live album, *The Blues—A Real Summit Meeting*.

Her sister, Mattie Fields, took Thornton under her care as her health continued to deteriorate in the early 1980s. On July 25, 1984, suffering cirrhosis of the liver, Thornton died of a heart attack. The one-time 350-pound blues singer had dwindled to a meager 95 pounds at her death. Most sources report that Thornton died alone and destitute, but at least two sources rely on secondhand accounts that claim she died in the presence of loved ones. Bandleader and reverend Johnny Otis presided at the funeral.

Thornton was inducted into the Blues Hall of Fame the same year she died. Her life later inspired the play *Howlin' Blues & Dirty Dogs: The Life of Big Mama Thornton*, by Theatre Perception Consortium writers Larry James Robins, Carla DuPree Clark and Tu'Nook. Jill Scott portrayed the blues singer in the 2007 movie *Hounddog*.

Vera Hall Ward,
Rich Amerson and
Dock Reed

Without John Lomax's work for the Library of Congress in the early twentieth century, few outside Alabama would have ever heard the voices of Adele Vera Hall or Dock Reed. Hall was born into a poor family in 1902, but the family did relatively well in comparison to many others, raising produce and livestock enough on their Sumter County farm to market for income and to feed themselves. The third of four children, Hall loved to sing and learned many gospel songs from her mother, Agnes, a former slave, and her father, Efron "Zully" Hall. In 1948 interviews with Lomax's son, Alan, Hall said that her mother sang "all the time," especially when cooking and cleaning.

Hall became locally well known for her singing, blending what she'd learned from her parents with what Rich Amerson taught her about blues and folksongs. Amerson, a lay preacher, drifter and singer born in Sumter County in 1893, was known for his colorful lifestyle, wearing his hair long, preaching the gospel, playing harmonica, singing beautifully and improvising wild tales in both song and speech. He easily charmed Lomax to include him on several compilations, most now out of print, but a CD of Amerson's recordings, *Selected Songs and Stories*, has been issued by the Alabama Folklife Association.

By age eleven, Hall provided child care for county families for income, and at age sixteen while traveling with one of the families, she met Nels Riddle of Tuscaloosa, who would become her first husband. She gave birth to a daughter in 1918, but the marriage ended in the early 1920s when her husband was shot and killed during a fight. Hall then worked as a cook and washerwoman in Tuscaloosa until the Great Depression, when she returned to Sumter County. After her daughter died from chronic hepatitis in 1940, Hall took in the sons of her sister, Minnie Ada.

Hall's cousin, Zebadiah "Dock" Reed, born in 1898 in Sumter County, often sang gospel duets with Hall, but it was Reed who most followed their Baptist upbringing, refusing to perform the "devil's music," defined as any song other than gospel. But when her mother died, Hall found that the blues provided some level of comfort. She began frequenting the Tin Cup area in Livingston, a popular Saturday night destination for juke joint entertainment, where she expanded her repertoire to include blues and work songs. Hall has since been compared to Lead Belly and Jelly Roll Morton for the size of her repertoire and the artistry with which she delivered traditional songs and blues. It was in Tin Cup where she met Willie Ward, a railroad worker from Greensboro, who is credited for teaching her many of the working songs and blues tunes she included in her repertoire.

Lomax met Hall in 1937 as a result of Sumter County folklorist Ruby Pickens Tartt. Hall's ability to memorize a song after hearing it only once amazed Lomax. She had an uncanny ability for improvisation with a voice that Lomax called one of the "loveliest" untrained voices he'd ever recorded. The recordings that Lomax and Tartt made inspired other ethnomusicologists to travel to Sumter, most seeking out Hall. Her fame spread internationally in the 1940s, when the British Broadcasting Corporation played her recording of "Another Man Done Gone." In 1945, Byron Arnold, a UA music professor, recorded Hall performing songs that were later released in a multi-artist collection. In 1948, she recorded more for Alan Lomax, who also interviewed her extensively, using the information to portray her in a 1959 fictional biography entitled *The Rainbow Sign*. In the 1950s, Harold Courlander recorded both Hall and Reed singing spirituals for the American Folkways Collection.

Reed loved children, but he and his wife Hattie were childless, though they took in his sister's two children when she died. Through the years, he teamed up with Hall to record for Lomax and other ethnomusicologists. Some of the recordings were later issued on the CD *Alabama: From Lullaby to Blues* in Rounder label's *Deep River Song* series. The Library of Congress also has other recordings available. In 1942, Reed developed problems with one of his feet, and in 1944, the leg had to be amputated below the knee. Lomax and Tartt helped him financially during that time, deepening an already respectful and affectionate relationship between Lomax and Reed. When Lomax died in 1948, it deeply affected Reed. As Reed mourned, Tartt showed him the words that Lomax had used to close his autobiography, words from a song that Reed had sung for Lomax: "Weep like a willow, moan like a dove,/ You can't get to heaven without you go by love." That purportedly provided solace for Reed. When Tartt died in 1974, Reed sang "Steal Away, Steal Away Home" at her funeral. Reed died on January 4, 1979, and is buried in Old Shiloh Cemetery near Livingston.

Hall faded into obscurity after release of *The Rainbow Sign*. She continued to work as a washerwoman and cook even as her vision grew worse due to cataracts. The fame from the earlier recordings resulted in little monetary income, and she died blind and indigent on January 29, 1964. She was buried in Livingston's Morning Star Cemetery, but the grave location was lost after the wooden cross marking it was bulldozed away during the 1970s. Hall's fame resurged in 1999 when techno-artist Moby incorporated Hall's vocal into a new rendition of "Trouble So Hard." Since her death, she has been inducted into the Alabama Women's Hall of Fame, and the Sumter County Historical Society and Alabama Blues Project have erected a memorial adjacent to the Sumter County Courthouse square to honor her contributions to music.

Dinah Washington

D ubbed "Queen of the Jukebox" and "Queen of the Blues," Dinah
    Washington lived a life no single adjective can describe adequately,
a life desperately hard and tragically short with experiences enough to fill
a dozen lifetimes, good and bad. Born Ruth Lee Jones in Tuscaloosa on
August 29, 1924, Washington became one of the most admired and critically
controversial artists of the twentieth century. Reminiscent of their reaction
to Nat King Cole, who switched from jazz piano to smooth pop vocal music,
critics attacked Washington for excelling in a range of musical genres, from
R&B and jazz to blues and pop.

Washington grew up in Chicago, playing piano and eventually directing her
church choir. While her father gambled and her mother worked to support
the family, Washington found refuge at her church, where she gave solo gospel
recitals by age ten and performed with choirs at other Chicago churches,
leading to an invitation to join the Sara Martin Singers to tour the gospel
circuit. At fifteen, she won a talent contest singing an R&B song at Chicago's
Regal Theater, and offers from R&B bands flooded in. Due to her age, though,
she declined the offers. Even so, she began sneaking out at night to perform
solo at clubs, taking a job as a pianist and singer at the Garrick Bar in 1942.
When talent manager Joe Glaser heard her, he put her in touch with Lionel
Hampton, who recruited her for his band in 1943. Hampton later claimed
that he gave the former Ruth Jones the name Dinah Washington, but other
sources credit Glaser. Washington's mother strongly disapproved of nightclub
performing, which led Washington to leave home and marry John Young, but

Dinah Washington.
Courtesy of the Alabama Music Hall of Fame.

she still maintained close contact with her family and shared her earnings from performances with them without telling them how she'd earned the money.

Despite her immense talent, her volatile temper and many marriages and affairs sometimes overshadowed her professional achievements, but her ability couldn't be ignored. Vocally, she was tonally perfect. Bandleader Mitch Miller once said that "she was a natural, bottomless talent." Writing about her in his autobiography, *Q*, Quincy Jones said that "she could take the melody in her hand, hold it like an egg, crack it open, fry it, let it sizzle, reconstruct it, put the egg back in the box and back in the refrigerator, and you would've still understood every single syllable."

After three years with Hampton's band, Washington decided to go solo, signing with Mercury Records, which led to a string of R&B hits beginning in 1950, including "I Wanna Be Loved," "I'll Never Be Free" and "I Only Know." Though she was the bestselling female R&B artist at the time, her recordings failed to cross over to white audiences, primarily because of Mercury's targeted marketing to African American audiences, denying her the same crossover notoriety that other African American artists such as Lena Horne and Nat King Cole enjoyed.

Musical Heritage from the Heart of Dixie

In 1954, her album *After Hours with Miss D.* received rave reviews as a jazz album from *Billboard*, *Down Beat* and *Metronome* magazines. Her follow-up, *Dinah Jams*, solidified her standing in the jazz world. At the 1958 Newport Jazz Festival, she appeared with Max Roach to underscore that she could no longer be considered a "race" artist and that she'd broken through the barriers. Her hit singles defied category, ranging from blues and jazz to pop. In 1959, her single "What a Diff'rence a Day Makes" rose to the pop chart's Top 10 and won the R&B Grammy for best recording of 1959.

The hits continued into the 1960s with songs such as "Baby, You've Got What It Takes" and "A Rockin' Good Way," adding to her already massive ego. Washington was quick to declare herself "Queen of the Blues" to anyone, to everyone, and she didn't tolerate any perceived disrespect. One story places her in a Detroit nightclub when Carmen McRae performed Washington's "Love Is Here to Stay." Washington reportedly rose from her table, singing loudly with McRae, approached the bandstand and took the microphone from McRae to finish the song and berate the stunned McRae for singing it in the Queen's presence. Whether this and other stories are true is debatable, since Washington believed that all publicity was good publicity and regularly exaggerated facts and behavior.

Married seven times, Washington had many affairs, most with musicians in the band. But even with her ego and multiple affairs and marriages, she was extremely self-conscious about her weight. A heavy drinker, she tried numerous weight loss medications over the years that eventually led her to experiment with depressants and stimulants. Still, her shrewd business ability remained unaffected, and she'd grown quite wealthy by the mid-1950s, enough to help up-and-coming singers she deemed worthy, support two sons and finance college for her two sisters. For herself, she loved shoes, furs and cars—purchases that did not distract her for long from her preoccupation with weight. She would regularly take weight control pills, drink too much alcohol and then take more pills, having forgotten what she'd already taken. On December 14, 1963, she died from a heart attack brought on by an overdose of diet pills and alcohol. She was thirty-nine.

After her death, her popularity waned, mainly due to the rise of rock and roll and soul music. As her record label promoted new artists, it allowed most of her work to go out of print, reissuing only her later pop hits. Then came compact disc technology, and the record company reissued Washington's vast catalogue, which garnered immediate attention and honors. The U.S.

Post Office issued a commemorative stamp of the artist in 1993, and she was inducted into the International Jazz Hall of Fame in 1996 and the Rock and Roll Hall of fame in 1999. In 1998, her life was explored in Oliver Goldstick's musical *Dinah Was*. In 2008, the City of Tuscaloosa renamed a section of Thirtieth Avenue as Dinah Washington Avenue, with son Robert Grayson and three grandchildren on hand for the 2009 dedication ceremony.

Jolly "Little Whitt" Wells and Cleo "Big Bo" McGee

S uccess always takes time, but it took some forty years for Jolly "Little Whitt" Wells and Cleo "Big Bo" McGee to introduce their music to audiences outside Alabama. Wells, born in 1931 in Ralph, and McGee, born in 1928 in a house straddling the Alabama-Mississippi line near Emelle, Alabama, shared a lifelong friendship based on music, forming their first band in the 1950s to play juke joints and community events. McGee, who joked that his family could eat breakfast in Alabama and sleep in Mississippi without leaving the house, was a master blues harpist, the perfect accompaniment for Wells on guitar, playing a rough, earthy style of blues.

McGee's grandmother taught him to play the harp, but the youngster honed his skills in a closet where he could better hear the instrument as he played. He made his first stage appearance at age five and perfected his style over the years by listening to and adapting what he liked from other blues and country artists. Wells, meanwhile, developed a guitar style that readily blended with and supported McGee's harp.

Unable to get enough gigs to provide steady income, the men became truck drivers for the next four decades until retirement finally set them on the path to the musical fame that had earlier eluded them. Due to the national revival of traditional blues during the 1990s, the duo discovered an enthusiastic audience in younger listeners who craved the authenticity of live music and real instruments.

In 1995, they released their first album, *Moody Swamp Blues*, on Birmingham-based blues label Vent Records, finally taking their music

Little Whitt and Big
Bo. *Courtesy of the
Alabama Blues Project.*

outside Alabama. They quickly established themselves on the international
blues circuit, touring Europe as part of a multi-act show. The UK blues
magazine *Blueprint* named *Moody Swamp Blues* CD of the Year for the duo's
creativity in covers and original songs. During the tour, Bo and Whitt
performed on TV and radio, as well as in concert throughout Europe,
including England's Gloucester Blues Festival and Belgium's Annual Spring
Blues Festival.

Back in the States, similar popularity didn't come until an appearance at the
Chicago Blues Festival in 1997, but the fame proved short-lived, as domestic
interest in blues again began to wane. Both men remained important figures
in Alabama blues, however, involving themselves in prominent educational
projects that had them performing and teaching in schools around the state.
In 2002, the duo came to an abrupt and tragic end when McGee's twenty-
two-year-old stepson shot and killed him. Authorities charged the stepson
with murder.

Wells continues to play and teach, but not at the same level as before his partner's death. The duo had been, as one reviewer put it, "as comfortable together as honey and butter and every bit as smooth." But driving down Moody Swamp Road near Tuscaloosa, as album notes on their only CD suggest, a person still might find Wells in his yard, picking the blues for friends who've dropped by to "see who can tell the biggest lie."

Hank Williams and Tee-Tot Payne

He spent most of his brief life in physical and emotional pain to have it end tragically in the back seat of a Cadillac. The third and last child of Lon and Willie Williams, Hiram King Williams was born on September 17, 1923, in Mount Olive West. Unknown at the time, the child had been born with spina bifida, a congenitally malformed vertebra that would cause pain throughout his life. Of meager build, Williams shunned school sports in preference for music, his earliest influence coming from recordings of Jimmie Rodgers, a Mississippi country singer who blended blues guitar with yodeling. But Williams later credited Rufus "Tee-Tot" Payne, an African American whom he met after the family moved from Georgiana to Greenville, as his greatest influence.

Payne was born in Lowndes County in 1884 to former slaves. The family reportedly moved to New Orleans about 1890, affording the young Tee-Tot an environment awash in music, but little else is known about his childhood, the origin of his nickname or why he returned to Greenville to settle after his parents died. Reports of his life back in Greenville vary. According to some, he became a "society" musician, playing for white functions, but other accounts describe him as a hunched-back drugstore janitor and delivery person who played street music with an open cigar box for donations. Williams later said that Payne had been a janitor at a Greenville school who gave him guitar lessons. Another story has those lessons occurring on the front porch of the Williams family's Georgiana home during summer and *under* the house in winter, the two supposedly crawling to a roomy spot near

Hank Williams with Buddy Killen on bass. *Courtesy of the Alabama Music Hall of Fame.*

the fireplace to stay warm. Lilly, Hank's mother, reportedly provided meals to Payne in exchange for the guitar lessons, but Williams later told reporters that he paid whatever change he had for each lesson.

Despite the conflicting and extraordinary claims of various stories, Payne's true history is shaded in vague memories that recall him as either a solo artist or small bandleader, depending on the source. While all of the stories credit Payne with teaching guitar to Williams, Williams family members have also credited Payne with teaching Williams how to assert himself. Musically, Payne stressed the importance of keeping time with a good beat, which comes through in many of Williams's songs. Musicologists also note a blues element in many of Williams's songs and credit that to Payne as well. Williams returned to Greenville in August 1952 for a Greenville Homecoming performance in which he publicly acknowledged Payne's influence, a bold act in mid-1900s Alabama. He intended to look up the old man, only to discover that Payne had died on March 17, 1939, in a charity hospital in Montgomery and was buried in an unmarked pauper's grave in Montgomery's Lincoln Cemetery. A cemetery marker to honor Payne has since been erected, though the actual grave site remains unknown.

Growing up, Williams regularly took his guitar to school to play during lunchtime, telling his classmates that his greatest ambition was to play and sing professionally. When the family moved to Montgomery, Williams quit school at age sixteen and began appearing on WSFA in late 1936, becoming one of the station's most popular performers. With his mother driving them to gigs, Williams and his band, the Drifting Cowboys, played beer joints and regional shows, drawing big enough crowds by the early 1940s to garner Nashville attention, but his music reputation only slightly outweighed his growing reputation for drinking. To dampen increasing back pain from the spina bifida, Williams's intake of alcohol grew in proportion. Unable to quell the pain with alcohol alone, he later added morphine to the mix. His increasing dependence on alcohol caused music industry insiders to consider him an unsafe bet despite his growing regional popularity.

In 1943, he met Audrey Mae Sheppard from Pike County, Alabama. Mother of two-year-old daughter Lycrecia, Audrey learned to play upright

An early Christmas card photo. Audrey, Lycrecia, Hank Jr. and Hank Williams. *Courtesy of the Alabama Tourism Department.*

bass and joined Williams's band. She also served as band manager. She and Williams married in December 1944, the start of a combative relationship, in part due to Audrey's desire to develop her own singing career and in part due to her competition with Williams's mother for Hank's attention.

In 1946, Williams met Fred Rose who, with Roy Acuff, ran a publishing company. Rose wasn't interested at first in Williams as a performer, preferring to take him on as a songwriter, but that soon changed, and Rose arranged for Williams to record four songs for the Sterling label in December 1946. In March 1947, thanks to Rose, Williams signed with MGM, with "Move It on Over" his first MGM release, followed by "Honky Tonkin'" in 1948.

Williams was now close to national stardom, but it appeared that the harder he worked to succeed, the harder he fought to fail. He regularly showed up for gigs drunk, late or not at all, growing increasingly difficult to deal with until Rose ended their relationship and Audrey filed for divorce. But Williams somehow reconciled with both, and they began a campaign to get wider exposure for the singer. *Grand Ole Opry* officials didn't want to take a chance, but KWKH in Shreveport, Louisiana, signed him with *Louisiana Hayride*. The Saturday night program drew fifty thousand listeners across the South, but Williams's recent releases had failed to do well, with "I'm a Long Gone Daddy" the highest, charting at number six, "Mansion on the Hill" falling short of the Top 10 and four others not charting at all. Then came a song that Hank's friends said was a waste of time to record, but it was a song Williams believed in, a song that was recorded quickly at the end of a session and released in February 1949. By May, "Lovesick Blues" had hit number one, and it stayed there for sixteen weeks. The *Grand Ole Opry* could no longer ignore him, and he began performing on the show, expanding his writing to include gospel music, recording several songs under the pseudonym "Luke the Drifter."

In 1951, Williams underwent corrective surgery to alleviate his back pain, but post-surgery pain proved even worse. By 1952, his life was coming apart. Dependent on morphine and alcohol that did little to relieve the pain, Williams was often too inebriated to perform. Audrey filed for divorce for a second time, and Williams returned to Montgomery to live with his mother. Despite the private turmoil, his music did well, with "Honky Tonk Blues" peaking at number two and five subsequent singles—"Jambalaya," "Half as Much," Settin' the Woods on Fire," "You Win Again" and "I'll Never Get Out of This World Alive"—all reaching the Top 10.

Williams then moved in with Ray Price in Nashville. In May 1952, his divorce was finalized, and the judge awarded the house, child custody and half of all future royalties to Audrey. In August, the *Opry* fired him, telling him that he could return when he decided to sober up. His downward spiral pushed away his friends and the Drifting Cowboys. He continued to play the *Louisiana Hayride* for reduced wages, performing with local bands. In the fall of 1952, he met and married nineteen-year-old Billie Jean Jones Eshlimar after signing an agreement to support a child he'd fathered with girlfriend Bobbie Jett. Although he married Billie Jean in a private ceremony in Minden, Louisiana, on October 18, a promoter suggested they perform the ceremony twice more the next day at the New Orleans Civic Auditorium, charging an estimated fourteen thousand people two dollars each to attend.

Following the marriage, Williams began to experience "heart problems" and used various prescription drugs to treat himself, even as he continued to drink heavily. Contracted to play New Year's Day in Canton, Ohio, Williams scheduled to fly out of Knoxville on New Year's Eve, but bad weather forced the flight's cancellation. Williams then hired college student Charles Carr to drive him to Ohio. He injected himself with shots of B-12 and morphine and crawled into the back seat of his Cadillac with a bottle of whiskey. Hours later on New Year's Day 1953, West Virginia police pulled Carr over for speeding and discovered Williams dead in the back seat. He was twenty-nine.

Williams was buried three days later in Montgomery's Oakwood Cemetery, drawing an estimated twenty thousand mourners. Authorities moved Williams's body on January 17 to a spot in Oakwood Annex Cemetery that could later accommodate other family members. His ex-wife, Audrey, who died on November 4, 1975, is buried beside him.

The singer's music has earned scores of awards and continues to sell well, and his name is one of the most recognizable in country music. The last song released during his life provided one final irony: "I'll Never Get Out of This World Alive" charted number one the month he died. In subsequent years, MGM, armed with Williams's original demos, decided to overdub bands onto the bare recordings, a process that continued through the 1960s until all original recordings fell out of print. The original recordings were eventually reissued on CD in the 1980s.

AND MORE:
MINI-BIOGRAPHIES

———◆◆◆———

Michael Graham Allen

Since the 1970s, musician, historian and craftsman Michael Graham Allen has been one of the most influential driving forces in popularizing the craft and music of Native American flutes. Born in Tuscaloosa in 1950 and growing up in Decatur, Allen began his research of ancient New World flutes in 1975. A self-taught artist and musician, he quickly became a primary force in their revitalization and popularization. In 1981, Allen met and began collaborating with Dr. Richard Payne, a celebrated authority on and champion of the Native American flute. Their friendship and collaborations lasted until Payne's death in 2004. In 1986, Allen and musician/engineer Barry Stramp, together under the name Coyote Oldman, introduced the Native American flute to mainstream and alternative music markets around the world with the groundbreaking recordings *Night Forest* and *Tear of the Moon*. With music featured in films and TV programs worldwide and with thirteen albums to

Coyote Oldman's credit, including the 2011 release *Time Travelers*, Allen has turned his attention to ancient New World rim-blown flutes, including Anasazi, Mojave and Hopi flutes, reintroducing them to the general public through lectures at colleges and music events, performances and recordings. Meanwhile, his handcrafted flutes have become coveted favorites of musicians around the world and are offered through the website coyoteoldman.com. "I am entertained by the ancient and the futuristic, seeking something essential and simply human," Allen says

Michael Graham Allen. *Photo by Jim Harlan. Courtesy of Michael Graham Allen.*

about his work. "Building my own experimental flutes has heavily influenced my music and vice versa. Although my flutes are descendants of North American artifacts, they are becoming new American instruments through considerable experimentation and evolution. My workshop is a laboratory." Allen's music and flutes weave "a gentle spell of calm and profound peacefulness," according to John Diliberto, producer of *Echoes*, a program of New Age music featured on National Public Radio. Allen's music, Diliberto says, "echoes across the plains like a haunted memory carried on the winds of the past."

ERNIE ASHWORTH

Huntsville native Ernie Ashworth is best remembered for his songwriting ability, but the song that put him on top of the 1963 country charts and became his signature tune was a cover. Born in 1928, Ashworth began writing songs as a youngster. By 1948, he had joined the Tunetwisters band, appearing on Huntsville's WBHP before moving to Nashville to perform on WLAC and WSIX and write songs for other artists. He eventually became a staff writer for the Acuff-Rose publishing house, providing songs that occasionally crossed over to the pop charts for country artists such as Little Jimmy Dickens and Carl Smith. In 1955, with producer Wesley Rose's help, he signed with MGM as Billy Worth, but none of the six original singles he recorded for the label proved commercially successful, so he returned to Huntsville in 1957 to work at the Redstone Arsenal missile plant. In 1960, Rose helped him sign with Decca, and his first single, "Each Moment (Spent with You)," charted in the Top 5. His song "You Can't Pick a Rose in December" charted in the Top 10 that same year. But it was John D. Loudermilk's "Talk Back Trembling Lips" that gave Ashworth his only number one hit, earning him performances on the *Grand Ole Opry* and Most Promising Male Artist awards from *Billboard* and *Cashbox* magazines in 1963. Throughout the 1970s, Ashworth released a string of songs, with twelve reaching the Top 10. In 1989, he purchased WSLV radio in Ardmore, Tennessee, and continued to release occasional recordings that proved popular with traditional country listeners in Europe. In 2008, he was inducted into the Alabama Music Hall of Fame. He continued to perform and record until his death on March 2, 2009.

Azure Ray

Seven years passed between Azure Ray's critically acclaimed first album, *Hold On Love*, and their 2010 release, *Drawing Down the Moon*, but the lapse did not reflect a break in the duo's careers. Born in 1975 and 1976, respectively, Birmingham natives Orenda Fink and Maria Taylor met while attending the Alabama School of Fine Arts. They fronted the Little Red Rocket band in the 1990s, releasing two albums on Tim/Kerr records. They later moved to Athens, Georgia, to form the duo Azure Ray, incorporating both folk and electronic elements into their recordings. After signing with Saddle Creek Records, they lent their talents to other artists such as Moby and played in the Saddle Creek band Now It's Overhead. Following 2003's *Hold On Love*, Fink and Taylor pursued solo careers, with Taylor releasing three albums and a collaborative EP with Saddle Creek artist Andy LeMaster. Fink released two solo albums and a solo EP, an album with Art in Manila and an album with the pop duo O+S. In 2009, the women reunited as Azure Ray to release *Drawing Down the Moon* and began an extensive tour in promotion of the album. They continue to perform internationally and record for Saddle Creek.

Azure Ray's Maria Taylor and Orenda Fink. *Photo by Nick Asokan, courtesy of Azure Ray and Saddle Creek Records.*

BO BICE

Stories about drug-related arrests dogged Harold "Bo" Bice in 2004 during the fourth season of *American Idol* and the tour of competitors that followed. The Helena native had indeed been arrested for cocaine possession in Huntsville in 2001 and for marijuana and paraphernalia possession in Birmingham in 2003, but he had completed a drug diversion program that satisfied both arrests by the time of the competition. The stories proved to have little effect on his audience appeal, as he delivered each week's performance with soul, singing rock classics that included the Allman Brothers' "Whippin' Post," looking more like a 1960s refugee than a twenty-first-century performer. The contest ended with Bice in second place to Carrie Underwood, but the runner-up spot was good enough to secure a deal with RCA, which released the album *Real Thing* in December 2005. Although the album went gold, RCA dropped Bice, and he formed his own label, Sugar Money Records, to release *See the Light* in 2007 and *Different Shades of Blue* in 2010. He continues to record and tour.

Bo Bice. *Photo by and courtesy of Darlene Moore.*

Buddy Buie

Dothan native and songwriter Buddy Buie began his professional music career with Bill Lowry and the Classics IV in the mid-1960s, co-writing songs for the group with J.R. Cobb that included the hits "Spooky," "Stormy" and "Traces." His successes eventually led to the opening of his own recording studio in Doraville, Georgia, where he produced acts that included Roy Orbison and B.J. Thomas. Buie produced more than twenty top-of-the-chart hits during the 1960s before he and Cobb expanded their services to manage the Atlanta Rhythm Section, a band lauded for its focus on music rather than gimmicks. Buie continued to write songs for numerous artists throughout the 1980s and '90s, including "Mr. Midnight" for Garth Brooks and "Rock Bottom" for Wynonna Judd. An Alabama Music Hall of Fame inductee, Buie retired to Eufaula, Alabama, in 2003.

Jim Cavender

Huntsville native Jim Cavender, born in 1962, is a self-taught guitarist, bassist and drummer whose impeccable talent for writing, performance and production has him busy both behind and in front of the microphone. Adept

Jim Cavender. *Photo by Erin Smith, courtesy of Jim Cavender.*

145

in multiple musical genres, Cavender has performed with numerous bands and artists, including the Jungle, Then Again, the Snake Doctors, Bo Diddley, Chocolate Armenteros and Percy Sledge. Since 1986, Cavender has also spent time in the studio producing several albums, from the Jungle's self-titled jazz album, to Swine Cadillac's blues album *It Creeps Up on You*, to Then Again's rock album *Move to the City*. Other albums to his production credit include the jazz CD *Brothers* by Ken and Harry Watters and the rockabilly CD *Black Boots and a Suitcase* by Joshua Black Wilkins. Part of the independent trend, Cavender heads the label Startlingly Fresh Records. While serving in several Huntsville-based bands, including the Rolling Jazz Revue, Keith Taylor Trio and the Snake Doctors, Cavender also teaches jazz guitar at UA–Huntsville.

THE CIVIL WARS

While some bands purposely complicate their style, others simplify. The duo of Muscle Shoals native John Paul White and California native Joy Williams, better known as the Civil Wars, belongs to the latter group of artists. Performing live gigs without a backup band, the duo has filled a niche

The Civil Wars. *Photo by and courtesy of Bradley Burgess.*

for audiences craving intimacy and connection with performers. Having met in a songwriting camp in 2008, as a duo White and Williams now deliver what have been called dark and evocative songs rooted in folk, pop and rock. Their breakthrough song, "Poison & Wine," from their first EP by the same name, catapulted them into the national spotlight when it was featured on the television drama *Grey's Anatomy* and when Taylor Swift announced that she'd included it in her official iTunes playlist. Performing on NBC's *The Tonight Show* and featured multiple times on National Public Radio, the duo released its first album, *Barton Hollow*, in February 2010 on the Nashville-based Sensibility Music label.

Tommy Couch

Tuscumbia native Tommy Couch prepared for his career primarily through extracurricular activities while at the University of Mississippi in the 1960s, booking acts for local parties and dances. He continued to perform these tasks after graduation under the name of Malaco Attractions, a company he formed with brother-in-law Mitchell Malouf. They were soon joined by Wolf Stephenson in Jackson to promote concerts by Herman's Hermits, the Who and many others. In 1967, the company opened a recording studio to produce records by local songwriters and artists, including Mississippi Fred McDowell. By 1985, Malaco had grown large enough to purchase the Muscle Shoals Sound Studios and expand operations to Nashville and London, featuring artists as diverse as the Jackson Southernaires, the Williams Brothers, Bobby "Blue" Bland and Little Milton. In 1986, the company grew even more with the purchase of the gospel division of Savoy Records. As Malaco expanded its Christian recordings and artists' list, it issued a series of vintage jazz recordings by artists such as Duke Ellington and Lionel Hampton. In 2004, the company sold the Muscle Shoals Sound facility to a film production company after projects at the Shoals studio declined dramatically. Couch continues to serve as company president.

William Levi Dawson

Born in 1899 and the eldest of seven children, William Levi Dawson ran away from his Anniston home at the age of thirteen to enter Tuskegee

William Levi Dawson. *Courtesy of the Alabama Music Hall of Fame.*

Institute. Supporting himself monetarily through manual labor, he became a member of the Tuskegee band and orchestra, playing until 1921, when he left the school to continue studies at Washburn College in Topeka, Kansas, the Horner Institute of Fine Arts in Kansas City, Missouri, and the American Conservatory of Music in Chicago, graduating in 1927 with a master's degree in composition. He served as first trombonist in the Chicago Civic Orchestra from 1926 to 1930 and won several awards, including the 1930 Wanamaker Contest prizes for song and orchestral compositions. In 1931, he returned to Alabama to head the School of Music at Tuskegee Institute, leading the Tuskegee choir to national fame and serving until 1955. In 1956, the U.S. Department of State sent him to Spain to conduct various choral ensembles for that country. The most famous of Dawson's compositions is the *Negro Folk Symphony*, on which he began working while in Chicago. The Philadelphia Orchestra, led by Leopold Stokowski, premiered the work in 1934. His many awards include the Marshall Bartholomew Award from the Intercollegiate Music Council and the Heinecke Award from the Society of European Stage Authors and Composers. He died in Montgomery on May 2, 1990.

William Lee Golden

Born in 1939, Brewton native William Lee Golden secured his place in music history in 1964 by providing baritone vocals for the gospel group the Oak Ridge Boys. The group produced a string of gospel and secular hits over the years, including "You're the One" and "Elvira." As other group members donned a more conservative appearance during the early 1980s, Golden stuck out with his long hair, beard and casual style, leading the others to vote him out of the group in 1985. With the help of Booker T. Jones and Joe Walsh, he recorded the solo album *American Vagabond*, containing two songs that made the country charts. He then began recording with two of his sons, and in 1995, the Oak Ridge Boys invited him back into the group. While continuing to perform with the Oak Ridge Boys and as a solo artist during the first decade of the twenty-first century, Golden turned much of his creative energy to painting. The

William Lee Golden. *Photo by and courtesy of Nathan Malone.*

recipient of numerous awards, including Alabama Music Hall's Lifetime Achievement Award and the Cherokee Indian Association's Entertainer of the Year Award, Golden has exhibited his paintings around the country in venues such as the Tennessee State Museum and Tulsa's Gilcrease Museum of Art.

VERN GOSDIN

During his long career, he became known as "the voice," thanks to a distinctive emotional delivery. Born in 1934, Woodland native Vern Gosdin began his singing career as a young teen in a gospel quartet while idolizing such artists as the Blue Sky Boys and the Louvin Brothers. He later moved with his family to Birmingham to host the local radio show *The Gosdin Family Gospel Show*. In 1961, Gosdin and his brother Rex moved to Long Beach, California, where they performed bluegrass with the Golden State Boys, featuring future Byrds member Chris Hillman. By 1967, Vern and Rex had left the group

Vern Gosdin. *Courtesy of the Alabama Music Hall of Fame.*

to perform again as a duo and had a Top 40 hit with "Hangin' On." They moved then to Atlanta, and Vern cut a two-song demo with Emmylou Harris in 1976, securing a recording deal with Elektra as both songs—"Yesterday's Gone" and a remake of "Hangin' On"—made the country Top 20. Gosdin recorded a few more hits by the end of the 1970s and moved to Nashville-based Compleat Records in 1980. He teamed with Max D. Barnes to release Top 10 songs over the next few years, including "If You're Gonna Do Me Wrong (Do It Right)" and "Way Down Deep" in 1983. In 1984, he had his first number one song with "I Can Tell by the Way You Dance (You're Gonna Love Me Tonight)." With the traditionalist revival during the late 1980s, Gosdin continued to do well on the charts, hitting number one with "Set 'Em Up, Joe" in 1988. "Chiseled in Stone," co-written with Barnes, won the 1989 Country Music Association's Song of the Year Award, the same year he released *Alone*, a country-style concept album chronicling the breakup of his marriage. During the 1990s, his popularity waned as country became more influenced by rock. He continued to record and perform until age seventy-four, when he suffered a stroke and died in April 2009.

Coot Grant

She was born in Birmingham circa 1893 as Leola B. Pettigrew, but she had adopted the stage name of Coot Grant by age twelve, when she teamed up with Chicago musician Wesley Wilson, better known as Kid Wilson, in 1905. Performing in vaudeville, traveling shows and revues, the couple married in 1912 and appeared under a number of billings, including Grant and Wilson, Hunter and Jenkins and Kid and Coot. They recorded with such artists as Louis Armstrong and Sidney Bechet and even appeared along with many others, including Billie Holiday, in the 1933 film *Emperor Jones*, starring Paul Robeson. The duo composed more than four hundred songs during their career, including "Gimme a Pigfoot and a Bottle of Wine" (recorded by Bessie Smith), "Dirty Spoon Blues," "I Don't Want that Stale Stuff" and "Dem Socks Dat My Pappy Wore." Coot also recorded with guitarist Blind Blake in 1926. Following the Great Depression and subsequent years during which the couple apparently made no recordings, they signed with King Jazz in the mid-1940s. By the 1950s, health problems forced Wilson to retire, but Coot reportedly continued to perform, although little or no further information about her later career, life or death exists.

URBIE GREEN

Trombonist Urbie Green is indisputably one of jazz's greatest musicians, a "trombonist's trombonist." Born Urban Clifford Green in 1926, the youngest of three brothers with a younger sister, the Mobile native has had an extensive career as a freelance trombonist, working with Woody Herman, Gene Krupa, Frankie Carle, Count Basie, Frank Sinatra, Leonard Bernstein, Miles Davis, Billie Holiday, Aretha Franklin and many others. Switching to trombone with a brother's hand-me-down after years of piano lessons from his mother, he joined the Auburn Knights University jazz band while still in high school and began working with the Tommy Reynolds Band at age sixteen. He was on the road by age seventeen with Bob Strong's Band. In 1947, praise from fellow musicians landed him a three-year stint with Gene Krupa's group. In 1950, he joined Woody Herman's Third Herd. By 1954, he'd become one of the most sought-after trombonists for recording and club work in New York City and is perhaps the world's most

Urbie Green. *Courtesy of the Alabama Jazz Hall of Fame.*

recorded trombonist, with more than forty albums in his name. Over the years, he's also worked with Martin trombone engineers to innovate hand-brace and slide comfort on trombones, create an improved water hole and design a chrome-plated goose neck to prevent marking of players' clothes by brass. Green is a 1995 inductee of the Alabama Jazz Hall of Fame. The Smithsonian Institute National Museum of American History Jazz Masters Program produced a documentary in 2009 on Green's life and contributions to jazz. Green's oral history is part of the national record housed at the museum's Archive Center. Residing in Pennsylvania, Green continues to perform at the Deer Head Inn and the annual Celebration of the Arts Festival in Delaware Water Gap, Pennsylvania.

MARY GRESHAM

Mary Gresham did a lot of studio work in Muscle Shoals during the 1960s, but it took four decades before she was "discovered." Born in 1943 in Selma, she began performing in a Baptist church as a young girl and fell in love with singing. When her family relocated to Fort Walton Beach, Florida, her brothers assembled a band that she fronted at age sixteen. The band eventually broke up, and Mary married soul vocalist Charles "Chuck" Cooper. The couple toured with the Wesley-David Mastersound during the late 1960s before settling in Atlanta. Shortly after the birth of their daughter, the couple split in 1971, and in 1973 Gresham moved to Muscle Shoals, where she began singing backup on various recording sessions. Wide recognition didn't come until 2008, when Soulscape released *Mary Gresham: Voice from the Shadows—The Story of a Muscle Shoals Soul Sister*, containing twenty-four tracks recorded primarily at FAME, Muscle Shoals Sound, Widget and Broadway studios between 1968 and 1977. The album resulted from chance when Soulscape founder Garry Cape heard various tracks in the Malaco Records archives. The archive tracks did not identify the singer, and it took more than a year for Cape to discover the singer's identity and begin putting the album together. Only four of the tracks had been released prior. Gresham continues to perform in the Muscle Shoals area.

JOE GUY

Joe Guy's career was bright and brief, a musical meteorite that burned out long before it should have. Born in 1920, the Birmingham native and disciple of Roy Eldridge had a promising career as a trumpeter, playing in Teddy Hill's Orchestra by age eighteen and later in the bands of Lucky Millinder, Charlie Barnet and Cootie Williams. Then he met Billie Holiday in the mid-1940s at the height of her career and the point when she was experiencing an emotional meltdown. Before she met Guy, she'd already developed an unhealthy craving for alcohol, marijuana and opium with her first husband, Johnnie Monroe. But after she and Guy married, things only worsened as the couple moved on to heroin use. Despite the drug use, the couple did well financially by running their own orchestra. In 1947, though, they were arrested separately for heroin possession. Although Holiday rebounded after an eight-month jail sentence, little more was heard from Guy after that. He died in obscurity at age forty-one in Birmingham.

FREDDIE HART

One of fifteen children in a sharecropping family that loved the *Grand Ole Opry*, Loachapoka native Freddie Hart, born in 1926 as Fred Segrest, worked long and hard before getting the recognition he craved. Playing guitar by age five, Hart took a job with a national work relief program at age twelve and at age fourteen falsified documents to join the U.S. Marines. He served in the Pacific during World War II, performing often in officers' clubs. After military service, Hart adopted his stage name to pursue a career in country music. He signed with Capitol Records in 1953 to record "Loose Talk," an original song that went to number one for Carl Smith. In 1956, Hart went to Columbia Records and began appearing regularly on the *Town Hall Party* TV program, but the exposure did little for his recordings, although his songs did well when recorded by other artists. It wasn't until 1971, when his song "Easy Loving" hit the airwaves, that he achieved major recognition as the song climbed to number one and won the Country Music Association Song of the Year award. He followed with numerous charting songs, including the number one hits "My Hang-Up Is You," "Bless Your Heart," "Got the All Overs for You (All Over Me)," "Super Kind of Woman" and "Trip to Heaven." He wrapped up the 1970s as one of the decade's top twenty

Freddie Hart. *Courtesy of the Alabama Music Hall of Fame.*

country hit-makers, but his success on the charts ended with his 1987 song "Best Love I Never Had," peaking at seventy-seven. Hart was inducted into the Alabama Music Hall of Fame in 2001 and the Songwriters Hall of Fame in 2004. He's released several albums since 2000 and continues to tour and perform selectively in the United States and Europe.

HAYWOOD HENRY

Birmingham native Frank Haywood Henry earned the reputation as one of the swing era's best baritone saxophonists. Born in 1913, Henry learned clarinet and tenor sax before concentrating on baritone. He worked with a number of bands throughout his career, including the Bama State Collegians in 1930 and Erskine Hawkins's band from 1934 into the 1950s. Performing well into the 1980s, Henry performed with scores of artists, from Duke Ellington to Snub Mosley and Earl Hines. He played on more than one thousand rock and roll records during the 1950s and '60s, appearing anonymously on many hits. He recorded three albums as a bandleader: one for Davis Records in 1957, one for Strand in the 1960s and one for Uptown in 1983. He died on September 15, 1994.

TAYLOR HICKS

In 1995, Birmingham native Taylor Hicks entered Auburn University with plans to major in journalism, but he dropped out three years later to pursue music performance as a career. Adapting a singing style similar to the styles of Ray Charles and Sam Cooke, Hicks spent a full decade struggling to succeed, playing briefly in a band ironically called Passing Through before going solo to perform in clubs and bars while trying to land a record contract. The break he sought, even after self-producing two albums in 1997 and 2005, never materialized. Then came Hurricane Katrina in 2005 while he was in New Orleans, and he received a free flight voucher when the airlines cancelled his flight home. On impulse, he used the voucher to fly to Las

Taylor Hicks. *Photo by and courtesy of Michael F. O'Brien.*

Vegas, where *American Idol* was auditioning for its fifth season. Throughout the competition, Hicks developed a solidly committed fan base, and on the season's final show, he finally got the break he'd craved by becoming the fifth *American Idol* winner. Three weeks later, his first nationally released single, "Do I Make You Proud," debuted at number one on *Billboard*'s Hot 100 Singles. Since then, he's released *Early Works*, a compilation of work he wrote before his *Idol* win, and *The Distance* on his independent label, Modern Whomp. He's also published the memoir, *Heart Full of Soul: An Inspirational Memoir about Finding Your Voice and Finding Your Way*.

Jerome Hopkins

Pianist Jerome Hopkins was born in 1924 in Tuscaloosa and earned a master's degree in music education at Howard University in Washington, D.C. He developed a name for his extraordinary piano playing as he backed blues vocalist George Craft at the OffBeat club in Washington, D.C. In 1956, Billie Holiday hired him for her band, a gig that lasted three years. From there, he played until 1965 for the D.C. Howard Theater house orchestra, backing acts such as Sarah Vaughn, Redd Foxx and the Jewel Box Revue, a troupe of female impersonators and one male impersonator that proved a big draw wherever it played. After leaving the Howard Theater, Hopkins moved back to his family home in Tuscaloosa and continued to perform solo at various southern venues until his death due to cancer on July 25, 1986.

Matthew Houck

Toney native Matthew Houck grew up in the 1980s listening to his parents' country and folk albums. He bought his first guitar at age fourteen, started writing songs and hit the road when he was nineteen, playing mostly coffeehouses and putting out his first indie album, *Hipolit*, under the name Fillup Shack because, as he told one reporter, he was too shy to use his own name. He's long since learned how to handle that shyness and has shared the stage with such greats as Willie Nelson at Farm Aid. Now performing with his band Phosphorescent, Houck has released several albums since 2003, including *A Hundred Times or More* and *Aw Come Aw Wry*. But it was his 2007 release, *Pride*, that garnered wide critical praise and public interest.

Matthew Houck. *Photo by and courtesy of Neff Connor.*

He followed that with *To Willie*, a compilation of eleven songs by Willie Nelson, reinterpreting them in honor of his childhood songwriting hero, again receiving critical praise as well as personal compliments from Nelson. In 2010, Houck returned to his own music, releasing *Here's to Taking It Easy*, shifting from the country sound of *To Willie* to a more classic rock sound. Houck and his band are currently based in Brooklyn, New York, recording on the Dead Oceans Records label.

EDDIE LEVERT

Bessemer native Eddie Levert is probably best known for his work with the soul and pop group the O'Jays. Born June 16, 1942, Levert formed the Triumphs gospel group with Walter Williams during high school in Canton, Ohio. The group, changing its name to the Mascots, signed with King

Eddie Levert. *Courtesy of the George F. Landegger Collection of Alabama Photographs in* Carol M. Highsmith's America: Documenting the 21st Century, *Library of Congress, Prints and Photographs Division.*

Records and recorded four songs in 1961. Then Cleveland disc jockey Eddie O'Jay, for whom the group eventually changed its name to honor, helped the performers to develop closer harmonies and secure a deal with Imperial Records. Their first single, "Lonely Drifter," charted in the R&B Top 100. Levert co-wrote many of the O'Jays' songs, including "Don't Walk Away Mad," "Lonely Drifter" and "I Like to See Us Get Down." An Alabama Music Hall of Fame inductee, Levert continues to perform with the O'Jays in concert and at engagements such as the 2010 Washington, D.C. Rally to Restore Sanity and/or Fear, organized by comedians and political commentators Jon Stewart and Stephen Colbert.

Sammy Lowe and J.L. Lowe

Birmingham natives Samuel "Sammy" Lowe and James L. Lowe shared a certain passion and talent for music. Giving up the dream to play professional baseball, Sammy Lowe, born in 1918, eventually served as the chief arranger and composer for the Erskine Hawkins Orchestra for nearly twenty-two

J.L. Lowe. *Courtesy of the Alabama Music Hall of Fame.*

years, writing such hits as "Bearmash Blues," "No Soap" and "Raid the Joint." His 1946 arrangement of "I've Got a Right to Cry" for Birmingham vocalist Laura Washington did well on the charts. (The smoky-voiced Washington stopped performing during the 1950s to rear a family. She died in late 1990, a few years after returning to performing in the Birmingham area.) Sammy's career spanned several decades and included performances with Cab Calloway, Sammy Davis Jr., Al Hirt, the Isley Brothers, James Brown and many others. He died on February 17, 1993.

Sammy's brother, James, born in 1914, worked with several bands over the years, including Fess Whatley's Orchestra, the Ike Williams Orchestra and the Imperial Wings of Rhythm, but he is remembered most for his dedication to preserving Alabama's jazz heritage. He became the state's leading authority on the subject, but he wanted to make sure his knowledge lived on after he was gone. In 1978, he founded the Alabama Jazz Hall of Fame to honor Alabama's jazz musicians and preserve the rich history of Alabama's contributions to the genre. He died on July 23, 1998.

Lucky Millinder

Reared in Chicago, Anniston native Lucius Venable "Lucky" Millinder provided a vital link between the big band swing style and R&B, despite the fact that he reportedly could not play an instrument or read music. Born in 1900, Millinder started in music as an emcee, announcing bands at various dances, which led him to become a dancer and frontman by 1931. In 1932, he fronted the New York Orchestra and other bands until he took over the Mills Blue Rhythm Band in 1934. Possessing an acute talent for assembling gifted musicians and vocalists into notable successful units, he formed the Lucky Millinder Orchestra in 1940, featuring members such as Dizzy Gillespie and Bull Moose Jackson, proving especially popular in Harlem for music that provided a transition from swing to R&B. He signed the orchestra with Decca and produced four records that topped the charts between 1942 and 1945, including the song "When the Lights Go on Again," featuring Gillespie on trumpet. Millinder was quite the showman and relished the spotlight as the band toured various R&B venues during the late 1940s and into the early 1950s. In 1954, he signed with King records, but the heyday of his band had ended. The band managed to produce only a few minor hits on the label, and Lucky faded into obscurity. He died in New York City on September 28, 1966.

Lucky Millinder and his Rhythm Orchestra. *Courtesy of the Alabama Jazz Hall of Fame.*

HENRY PANION III

Born and reared in Birmingham, Henry Panion III has topped *Billboard*'s gospel and classical crossover charts with *Gospel Goes Classical*, featuring Juanita Bynum, Jonathan Butler and the GGC Symphony Orchestra Choir, but he may be best known for his work as conductor and arranger for Stevie Wonder. He's led numerous orchestras for Wonder in performance and recording, including the Royal Philharmonic, the Bolshoi Theater Orchestra, the Birmingham (England) Symphony and the Boston Pops. Panion received a BA in music education from Alabama A&M University and master's and doctorate degrees in music theory from Ohio State University. Panion has arranged and conducted for Wonder since 1992, and he has arranged and/or conducted for a wide range of other artists, including the Winans, Chet Atkins, the Blind Boys of Alabama, Aretha Franklin and Chaka Khan. The former director of the Birmingham Metropolitan Orchestra (1995–97) has produced work that's earned two Grammys and two Dove Awards, among many other awards, including induction into the Alabama Jazz Hall of Fame. In 2009, Panion was appointed cultural ambassador for the city of Birmingham.

SUSANNA PHILLIPS

Born in 1981, Birmingham native Susanna Phillips has fully established herself in the world of opera, having received numerous awards, including Metropolitan Opera's 2010 Beverly Sills Artist Award. After graduating high school in Huntsville, she attended New York's Juilliard School, where she garnered national attention in 2005 by winning four international vocal competitions, including Operalia, the Metropolitan Opera National Council Auditions, the MacAllister Awards and the George London Foundation Awards. She debuted at the Metropolitan Opera in 2008, playing Musetta in *La Boheme*. Since then, she has played several roles in Met productions, including Pamina in *The Magic Flute*, and in productions with other companies, including Opera Birmingham and the Boston Lyric Opera. She has also appeared often in solo recital since her New York solo debut in 2009 at Lincoln Center's Alice Tully Hall as the recipient of the Alice Tully Vocal Arts Debut Recital Award. She has performed with numerous symphonies, including the Royal Stockholm Philharmonic, Santa Fe Symphony, Santa Barbara Symphony and the New York Pops. She regularly returns to Alabama for recitals and orchestral appearances.

RAY REACH

Born in 1948, Birmingham native Raymond E. Reach has devoted much of his life to the promotion of music by Alabama jazz musicians. Beginning with piano at age six, Reach went on to study music at the Birmingham Conservatory of Music, Birmingham-Southern College (BSC), University of Montevallo (UM) and UA. In the late 1960s, Reach worked as a Muscle Shoals studio musician before turning his attention to academia during the 1970s, creating jazz workshops at BSC and courses and workshops at UM, UA and the University of North Texas. From 1998 through 2005, Reach served as instructor of jazz and music technology at UA–Birmingham and has since served as director of Student Jazz Programs at the Alabama Jazz Hall of Fame. Reach has also established himself as an in-demand performer, directing the Magic City Jazz Orchestra (MCJO) and appearing with a diverse range of artists, from Clark Terry and Dizzy Gillespie to Cleveland Eaton and Ellis Marsalis. The founder and CEO of Magic City Music Productions, he began production work in 2010 on the MCJO CD *Spinning Wheel: The Magic City Orchestra Plays the Music of Blood, Sweat, and Tears.*

WILLIE RUFF

Willie Ruff is respected as much for his research in ethnomusicology as he is for his French horn and bass musicianship. Born in 1931, the Sheffield native joined Lionel Hampton's band soon after graduation from Yale University and later formed the Mitchell-Ruff Duo with his friend Dwike Mitchell, performing with such jazz giants as Louis Armstrong, Count Basie and Dizzy Gillespie. In 1959, the duo took jazz to the Soviet Union, where they taught and performed in Russian conservatories. In 1981, they taught and performed in China. Ruff has served on the faculties of Yale School of Music (since 1971), UCLA, Dartmouth and Duke University. He is the founding director of the Duke Ellington Fellowship program at Yale. Academically, Ruff's research examining the roots of gospel has provided some unexpected results. Based on the data he's collected, Ruff has concluded that the music of black American churches has more in common with the Gaelic music of Scotland than it has with music traditions of Africa. His 1992 memoir, *A Call to Assembly*, won the Deems Taylor ASCAP award. He continues to teach at Yale and perform as part of the Mitchell-Ruff Duo.

RAY SAWYER

In 1967, a car accident took Chickasaw native Ray Sawyer's right eye and put him in a wheelchair for a year. This was a bit of horrible luck that would one day prove an asset. Born in 1937, Sawyer became a professional musician at age fourteen as the drummer of a local band. Following the car accident, he began sporting an eye patch that eventually became his trademark. In 1968, he traveled to Union City, New Jersey, where he and local singer-songwriter Dennis Locorriere teamed up with two Mississippi musicians and a New Jersey drummer to form a no-name bar band. One club owner finally demanded a name for posters, and the band members came up with Dr. Hook and the Medicine Show, derived mainly from Sawyer's distinctive eye patch. Their first break came when they were asked to perform the Shel Silverstein song "Last Morning" for the film *Who Is Harry Kellerman and Why Is He Saying Those Things About Me?*, leading to a contract with CBS and a move to San Francisco. Their first hit, "Sylvia's Mother," another Silverstein song, didn't make an impression initially, but CBS redoubled promotional

Ray Sawyer. *Photo by and courtesy of Jeff Ziff, aka Sodafixer.*

efforts, eventually sending the song to the top of the charts. The song the band is most remembered for is yet another by Silverstein, "The Cover of the *Rolling Stone*," which resulted in the band's appearance on the *Rolling Stone* cover. The band had a few more hits through the decade, with their last major hit, "Sexy Eyes," in 1980. The group disbanded in 1985. Backed by different musicians, Sawyer continues to perform and record as Dr. Hook featuring Ray Sawyer. A 2005 Alabama Music Hall of Fame inductee, Sawyer released his fifteenth album, the autobiographical *Captain*, in 2010.

THE SECRET SISTERS

Praised for their haunting harmonies and natural sound, sisters Lydia and Laura Rogers stepped onto the national stage at a 2009 Nashville audition, their performance drawing the immediate attention of producer T. Bone Burnett and rocker Jack White. That attention quickly led to the recording of the sisters' first album, *The Secret Sisters*, taking only two weeks to complete.

The Secret Sisters, Lydia and Laura Rogers. *Photo by and courtesy of James Noblitt Thigpen.*

Critics and audiences alike laud the duo for intricate harmonies that hint influences of rural music from the 1920s. Born two years apart in the mid-1980s, the Muscle Shoals natives have adopted a retro style not only in their voices but also in their clothing and hairstyles, which are more appropriate to the early to mid-1900s than the early twenty-first century, as they perform classic folk, country, pop and bluegrass songs to critical and audience acclaim. Since the release of their first album, they've taken their act of a single guitar and dual vocal harmonies on the road, sharing the stage with such stars as Chris Thile, Elvis Costello and Willie Nelson.

TOMMY SHAW

Born in 1953, Montgomery native Tommy Shaw has written some of classic rock's most enduring songs, including "Fooling Yourself" and "Too Much Time on My Hands" for the group Styx. Shaw joined Styx in 1975 to replace the group's departing guitarist, John Curulewski. In the mid-1980s, Shaw

Tommy Shaw. *Photo by and courtesy of Todd Evans.*

released three moderately successful solo projects before joining with Ted Nugent in 1987 in the group Damn Yankees, whose self-titled album went platinum. Unable to sustain fan interest with the second album, the group disbanded, and Shaw reunited in 1996 with Styx to tour and record an album of new material, the first for the band in fifteen years. While continuing both solo and Styx work in 2007, Shaw and former Damn Yankees member Jack Blades released *Influence*, a compilation of songs that had influenced each of the musicians during their careers. The recipient of numerous awards, including induction into the Alabama Music Hall of Fame, Shaw showed another side to his talent in 2011 with the release of the bluegrass-oriented album *The Great Divide*.

Tommy Stewart

Arguably one of the most influential people in Tommy Stewart's childhood was his mother, a songwriter, vocalist and choir conductor, so his interest in music as a career probably surprised few who knew him. Born in 1939, he was already performing in the high school marching band by age ten and was later voted by his peers as most likely to succeed in music. Stewart began a career that spanned five decades by studying with Fess Whatley and arranging for and performing with an array of artists, including Wynton Marsalis, Isaac Hayes, Lou Rawls, John Coltrane and many others. The cofounder of the African American Philharmonic Orchestra, he has issued numerous recordings, including *Tommy Stewart and His Orchestra* and the 1973 Buddha Records recording *The Burning of Atlanta*. His most famous album, however, may be the self-titled *Tommy Stewart* from 1976, featuring the song "Bump and Hustle Music," the one song on the album he reportedly thought would be the least liked by listeners, but it has proved to be one of the most popular. Stewart was inducted in 1988 into the Alabama Jazz Hall of Fame, where he serves as a member of the jazz faculty.

Gene Sullivan

Born in 1914 in Carbon Hill, Gene Sullivan set himself into a first career that was as far away from music as one can get—professional boxing. Then, in 1932, he abruptly quit the fight trade and bought a guitar with the aim

Gene Sullivan. *Courtesy of Eric Siegmund.*

to become a country music star. When he'd learned to play well enough, he joined a band called the Tune Wranglers for a short time, followed by the Lone Star Cowboys, playing on KWKH in Shreveport, Louisiana. He left the band to form a duo with Florida native Wiley Walker in 1939 and work at radio stations in Fort Worth, Lubbock and Oklahoma City. In 1941, the duo recorded "When My Blue Moon Turns to Gold Again," achieving some local success, but it was Elvis Presley's version in 1956 that made the song popular. The duo's only chart success was "Make Room in Your Heart for a Friend," reaching number two on the country chart. They appeared as featured regulars on Oklahoma City TV stations throughout the late 1940s before breaking up in the early 1950s. As a solo artist, Sullivan charted in 1957 with a comedy song entitled "Please Pass the Biscuits," a demo he'd recorded for Little Jimmie Dickens, but the record company preferred Sullivan's version over Dickens's. Sullivan then went into semi-retirement to run an Oklahoma City music store, but he continued to appear occasionally with Walker into the early 1960s. After Walker died in 1966, Sullivan continued to perform until his death in 1984.

THE THRASHER BROTHERS

Heflin natives Jim, Buddy and Joe Thrasher received their first national exposure when they were children, performing on the *Wally Fowler Gospel Sing* at the *Grand Ole Opry* in 1948. Five years later, they won *Ted Mack's National Talent Show* and toured with Mack's group for the next two years. Over the next two decades, their rich harmonies established them as one of gospel music's most popular groups, leading to the production and hosting of the TV show *America Sings* from 1967 through 1976, the year they recorded their most popular song, "One Day at a Time." In the early 1980s, they ventured into pop and country to deliver the hit "Still the One." With Jim

The Thrasher Brothers. *Courtesy of the Alabama Music Hall of Fame.*

and Joe having founded Thrasher Brothers Tours (a motor-coach company) in 1969, the brothers retired from music in 1986. The Thrasher Brothers came out of musical retirement in 1996 to record *The Thrasher Brothers Encore* for Homeland Records, featuring several star bass singers, including George Younce, J.D. Sumner and Brock Speer, as well as a 1971 recording of the group's now-deceased original bass singer, John Gresham. The Thrasher Brothers have won a Dove Award and four Grammys and are Alabama Music Hall of Fame inductees.

THE TRENIERS

With twin brothers and Mobile natives Claude and Cliff Trenier serving as frontmen, the Treniers group is considered by many critics to be the critical link between the swing music of the 1930s and '40s and rock and roll of the 1950s as they merged swing into blues during the late 1940s. That blending of swing and blues led directly to the development of rock and roll during the 1950s. With solid beats, manic sax solos and song titles like "Rocking on Sunday Night," the group's music influenced many of the rockers who came to prominence during the 1950s, artists that included Bill Haley, who

The Treniers. *Courtesy of the Alabama Music Hall of Fame.*

had seen the Treniers in performance when he was trying to succeed as a country artist. Not long after that performance, Haley switched gears and started rocking. While a direct influence on rock and roll's development, the Treniers' sound became more R&B oriented during the 1950s, even as they performed on TV programs such as the *Red Skelton Show* and made guest appearances in a few rock and roll movies, including *Don't Knock the Rock* and *The Girl Can't Help It*. Always dressing fashionably for performance, the Treniers became one of the first lounge acts in Las Vegas and opened occasionally for Frank Sinatra. Cliff died in 1983, and Claude died in 2003. Milt Trenier, joining with his older twin brothers in the group in 1951, continues to perform occasionally in Chicago.

MACK VICKERY

Born in 1938, Town Creek native Mack Vickery lost his mother when he was three and spent much of his young life moving from state to state with his father. He became serious about music after several positive experiences singing in high school assemblies—so positive that he lied about his age so he could sing in Ohio and Michigan bars. In 1957, he cut three songs for Sun Records, but Sam Phillips wasn't impressed enough to sign him, and the records remained unissued for two decades. Although he released a few records on small labels over the following years, it was in songwriting for others that he made his mark, first with "She Went a Little Bit Further," co-written with Merle Kilgore and becoming a hit for Faron Young in 1968. Others who recorded his songs included John Anderson, Johnny Paycheck, Willie Nelson, Vern Gosdin, Waylon Jennings and his hard-partying friend, Jerry Lee Lewis, who recorded several of Vickery's songs, including "Honky Tonk Wine," "Ivory Tears," "I Sure Miss Those Good Old Times" and the very suggestive "Meat Man." In 1989, Vickery won the *Music City News* Song of the Year award for "I'll Leave This World Loving You," which had been a hit for Ricky Van Shelton. He released only one album during his life, *Live! At the Alabama Women's Prison*, cited most often for its campy cover, which pictures Vickery in black boots, tight pants, a vest, a billowy-sleeved silk shirt and a scarf, with a guitar slung over his back as he sports a blond pompadour and poses before a dreary prison cell with three sensuous models locked inside, barefoot, wearing short skirts and their hair in beehives. Vickery died of a heart attack on

Mack Vickery. *Courtesy of the Alabama Music Hall of Fame.*

December 21, 2004. Bear Family Records subsequently reissued *Live! At the Alabama Women's Prison* on CD, featuring the full LP and two bonus tracks, including Vickery's version of "Meat Man."

MERVYN WARREN

In 1980, Huntsville native Mervyn Warren became a member of Take 6, an a cappella group that quickly achieved worldwide fame and propelled Warren to a career of music production and composition. Born in 1964, Warren possesses a broad musical talent for composing, producing and arranging, as well as a keen ability in both piano and vocals. He formed his first vocal group, the Symbolic Sounds, at age ten, performing original material and his arrangements of well-known gospel songs. After becoming a member of Take 6 at Oakwood College, he coproduced the group's first two albums, which resulted in four Grammy Awards. In 1991, he left the group to become a full-time producer and film music composer. In 1992, he won yet another Grammy, this time for producing the album *Handel's Messiah: A Soulful Celebration*. His work spans several genres, from pop and hip-hop to jazz and country, and he's worked with numerous artists, from DMX and Barbra Streisand to Quincy Jones and David Foster. He continues to work primarily as a record producer and composer of feature film music.

THE WATTERS BROTHERS

Huntsville natives Harry and Ken Watters have developed a special onstage rapport that perhaps only siblings can accomplish. With Harry on trombone and Ken on trumpet, they have repeatedly earned the praise of critics for both their live and recorded performances. The brothers have had their music featured on National Public Radio's *All Things Considered* and *Jazz South* and Public Radio International's *After Hours*. Graduates of the University of

The Watters Brothers.
Courtesy of the Watters Brothers.

North Texas, the brothers have established themselves as both band and solo artists. Harry has recorded with numerous artists, including Al Hirt, Peter Nero and Carl Fontana, and has been the featured soloist with various bands and orchestras. He currently serves with the U.S. Army Band in Washington, D.C., and teaches jazz trombone at George Mason University in Virginia. Ken performs wherever the music takes him and has worked with numerous artists, including Herbie Mann, Harry Connick Jr., Bobby "Blue" Bland, Gregg Allman and Frank Sinatra. He is currently based in Atlanta, Georgia.

COOTIE WILLIAMS

Trumpeter Cootie Williams became well known among musicians and audiences alike as a master of improvisation. Born Charles Melvin Williams in 1911, the Mobile native played various instruments in school bands before finally settling on trumpet and teaching himself to play. He toured with various bands before moving in 1928 to New York, where he joined Duke Ellington's band, playing a plunger-muted trumpet, demonstrating a more adept muting technique than that of Bubber Miley, the trumpeter he

Cootie Williams. *Photo by William P. Gottlieb, courtesy of the William P. Gottlieb/Ira and Leonore S. Gershwin Fund Collection, Music Division, Library of Congress.*

replaced. While with Ellington, Williams recorded with other artists as well, including Lionel Hampton, Teddy Wilson and Billie Holiday. An admirer of Louis Armstrong, Williams had a definitive way of placing emotion in his music, from intimate to harsh, and became noted for his ability to improvise. In 1940, Williams left Ellington's band and spent a year with Benny Goodman before leading his own big band throughout much of the 1940s. He then headed various R&B groups until he rejoined Ellington's band in 1962. Ellington even penned a tune called "New Concert for Cootie" specifically to feature the trumpeter. After Ellington's death, Williams played in the Mercer Ellington Band into the 1970s. He died in New York City on September 15, 1985.

Wet Willie

In 1969, a group of R&B-oriented musicians formed the band Fox, with Birmingham natives Jimmy Hall on vocals and sax and brother Jack on bass and banjo, Mobile natives Lewis Ross on drums and John Anthony on keyboards and Georgia native Rick Hirsch on lead and slide guitar. In 1970, the band moved to Macon, Georgia, where Capricorn Records cofounder and partner Frank Fenter changed their name to Wet Willie and signed the band to the Macon-based label, home to acts such as the Allman Brothers and Marshall Tucker Band. Wet Willie's style was different, though, more white soul than southern rock. Their first three albums did little commercially, but their fourth, *Keep on Smilin'*, provided their breakthrough hit, the album's title song. Subsequent releases, however, could not sustain the momentum of "Keep on Smilin'," and members began to depart from the band. Frontman Jimmy Hall later worked with several artists, including Dickey Betts and Jeff Beck. In 1981, he moved to Nashville and subsequently released several CDs, including *Triple Trouble* with Lloyd Jones and Tommy Castro. He currently fronts the band Deep South. Rick Hirsch, based now in California, continues to record for various projects. His latest CD release is *Instrumentality*. Bassist Jack Hall performs in the indie band Crosstown Allstars. Lewis Ross has been drumming for the Birmingham-based indie group Alabama Blues Machine. In the 1990s, Wet Willie's original core members, including Anthony on keyboards, reunited, and the band in various incarnations has since continued to perform. Wet Willie was inducted into the Georgia Music Hall of Fame in 1996 and the Alabama Music Hall of Fame in 2001.

And Finally...

Alabama's contributions to music are innumerable and profound, with many more artists past and present than one or several books can adequately cover—artists such as Jason Isbell (formerly of Drive-By Truckers), Clarence Carter, Jim Connor of the New Kingston Trio, Dean Jones, lyric soprano Irene Jordan, Jim Yester of the Association, Sandy Posey, Curly Putman and many, many others. For those who love the stories and history of music and the individuals who shape and develop the various genres, this book can serve only as a starting point on a journey of exciting discovery.

Selected Bibliography

Adams, Greg. "Freddie Hart." Country Music Television. www.cmt.com/ artists/az/hart_freddie/bio.jhtml.

Akenson, James E. "Alabama." Encyclopedia of Alabama. November 18, 2008. www.encyclopediaofalabama.org/face/Article.jsp?id=h-1865.

"Alabama: From Lullabies to Blues Deep River of Song: The Alan Lomax Collection. (Off the Beaten Track)." *Sing Out!* (Fall 2001): 118+.

Alabama State Council on the Arts. "Whitt Wells." *Carry On: Celebrating Twenty Years of the Alabama Folk Arts Apprenticeship Program.* N.p., 2008, 57.

"Alabama Sues Drummer Mark Herndon." Great American Country. June 9, 2008. www.gactv.com/gac/nw_headlines/ article/0,,gac_26063_5882375,00.html.

Ankeny, Jason. "Pinetop Smith." AllMusic. www.allmusic.com/artist/ pinetop-smith-p9700/biography.

Berntson, Ben. "Alabama Jazz Hall of Fame (AJHOF)." Encyclopedia of Alabama. January 22, 2009. encyclopediaofalabama.org/face/Article. jsp?id=h-2012.

Bessman, Jim. "Charlie Louvin." *Billboard*. July 14, 2007.

Bledsoe, Wayne. "Hank Day: Hank Williams's Light Never Stops Shining." *Knoxville News-Sentinel*, September 30, 2010.

"Bo Bice." Starpulse.com. www.starpulse.com/Music/Bice,_Bo/Biography.

Bolton, Jonathan W. "Sam Phillips." Encyclopedia of Alabama. December 3, 2010. www.encyclopediaofalabama.org/face/Article.jsp?id=h-2989.

Browne, Ray B. "An Alabama Songbook: Ballads, Folksongs, and Spirituals Collected by Byron Arnold." *Journal of American Culture* 28, no. 1 (2005): 132.

"Buddy Buie." Georgia Music Hall of Fame. www.georgiamusic.org/index. php?option=com_content&view=article&id=237&Itemid=63.

Bush, John. "William Lee Golden." Country Music Television. www.cmt. com/artists/az/golden_william_lee/bio.jhtml.

Cauthen, Joyce. "Charlie Stripling." Encyclopedia of Alabama. October 7, 2009. www.encyclopediaofalabama.org/face/Article.jsp?id=h-2473.

Chadbourne, Eugene. "Coot Grant." AllMusic. www.allmusic.com/artist/ coot-grant-p289584/biography.

Clarke, John. "Blues CDs." *The Times (London)*, February 27, 2004, 16.

Cobb, Buell E., Jr. *The Sacred Harp: A Tradition and Its Music*. Athens: University of Georgia Press, 1989.

Cooley, Billy Joe. "Thrasher Brothers Inducted into Alabama Music Hall of Fame." SouthernGospel.com. May 5, 2005. www.southerngospel.com/ Southern-Gospel-News/11591575.

Cooper, Dick. "Swampland: Johnson Family of Muscle Shoals." Swampland: Cultures of the South. January 2000. swampland.com/articles/view/ title:_johnson_family_of_muscle_shoals.

"Cootie Williams." Biography.com. www.biography.com/articles/Cootie-Williams-37123.

Corey, Russ. "A Lot Has Changed Since Song's Recording 50 Years Ago." *Times Daily (Florence, AL)*, February 22, 2007. www.timesdaily.com/apps/pbcs.dll/article?AID=2007702220302.

———. "Mary Mason Not Finished by Any Means." *Times Daily (Florence, AL)*, April 24, 2008. www.timesdaily.com/article/20080424/NEWS/804240302?Title=Mary-Mason-not-finished-by-any-means.

"Cow Cow Davenport." The Red Hot Jazz Archive. www.redhotjazz.com/cowcow.html.

"Coyote Oldman, Ancient North American Flutes and Flute Music." coyoteoldman.com.

"Coyote Oldman." Star's End Ambient Radio. www.starsend.org/coyoteoldman.html.

"Cybergrass Bluegrass Music News: Charlie Louvin Benefit Raises Over $20,000 To Aid Ailing Artist." Cybergrass, The Internet Bluegrass Music News Magazine. www.cybergrass.com/modules.php?name=News&file=article&sid=8198.

Dahl, Bill. "Eddie Kendricks." Encyclopedia of Alabama. February 8, 2010. www.encyclopediaofalabama.org/face/Article.jsp?id=h-2535.

"Dave Edwards." Welk Musical Family. June 1, 2006. welkmusicalfamily.blogspot.com/2006/06/dave-edwards.html.

Daveys, Colin. "Boogie-Woogie History." Boogie Woogie Festival. www.boogiegroove.ch/festival/history.htm.

Dennis, Paul W. "The Voice Remembered: A Tribute to Vern Gosdin." The 9513 | Country Music Blog. April 29, 2009. www.the9513.com/the-voice-remembered-a-tribute-to-vern-gosdin.

Dillon, Charlotte. "Cleveland Eaton." AllMusic. www.allmusic.com/artist/cleveland-eaton-p17228/biography.

"Dinah Washington." LyricsFreak.com. www.lyricsfreak.com/d/dinah+washington/biography.html.

"Dinah Washington: A Queen in Turmoil." National Public Radio: News & Analysis, World, US, Music & Arts. www.npr.org/templates/story/story.php?storyId=3872390.

Dreisbach, Tina S. "Willie Mae 'Big Mama' Thornton." Encyclopedia of Alabama. June 13, 2008. encyclopediaofalabama.org/face/Article.jsp?id=h-1573.

"Eddie Floyd." The History of Rock and Roll. www.history-of-rock.com/eddie_floyd.htm.

Eder, Bruce. "Wet Willie." ARTISTdirect Network. www.artistdirect.com/artist/bio/wet-willie/508893.

Elliott, Natalie. "Mary Gresham." Oxford American. December 1, 2010. www.oxfordamerican.org/articles/2010/dec/01/mary-gresham.

"Ernie Ashworth." Grand Ole Opry Star Ernie Ashworth. www.ernieashworth.com/bio.htm.

"Erskine Hawkins." Encyclopedia of Alabama. October 8, 2007. www.encyclopediaofalabama.org/face/Article.jsp?id=h-1365.

"FAME: Studio Rhythm Sections." FAME. www.fame2.com/studio-rhytm-section.

"Fed: US Ggroup 'Ripped Off' Prisoner Theme Tune: Musician." AAP News. find.galegroup.com/gps/infomark.do?&contentSet=IAC.

Ferguson, Benjamin. "Martha Reeves: The Motown Spirit Is Needed in Detroit Once Again." The Guardian. May 28, 2010. www.guardian.co.uk/music/2010/may/28/detroit-martha-reeves-motown.

Ferrari, Valerie. "Hank Williams' Alabama Grave." Associated Content. October 25, 2006. www.associatedcontent.com/article/74928/hank_williams_alabama_grave.html?singlepage=true&cat=16.

Flynt, Wayne. 2001. "Alabama's Shame: The Historical Origins of the 1901 Constitution." *Alabama Law Review* 53, no. 1 (2001): 67–76.

Fuqua, Christopher. *Music Fell on Alabama.* Huntsville, AL: Honeysuckle Imprint, 1991.

"Gaelic Gospel Music!" *Presbyterian Record*, November 2003, 12.

Gioia, Ted. "Handy's Version: There's a Story Behind the Story of 'St. Louis Blues.'" *Weekly Standard*, April 13, 2009.

Halli, Robert W. Jr. "Byron Arnold and the Folksongs of Alabama." Find Articles. findarticles.com/p/articles/mi_qa4113/is_200601/ai_n17180618.

Harvey, Alec. "Birmingham Native Hugh Martin Writes the Book on His Storied Composing Career." *Birmingham News*, October 24, 2010.

"Haywood Henry." MuseumStuff.com. www.museumstuff.com/learn/topics/Haywood_Henry.

"Henry Panion III." UAB Music Department. www.music.uab.edu/site2/panionbio.htm.

Hirshey, Gerri. "Wilson Pickett, 1941–2006." *Rolling Stone* 993 (2006): 17.

"Historic Muscle Shoals Sound Studios Closes." Billboard.com. www.billboard.com/bbcom/news/article_display.jsp?vnu_content_id=1000815532#/bbcom/news/article_display.jsp?vnu_content_id=1000815532.

"A History of Knighthood." The Auburn Knights Orchestra. www.auburnknights.com/history.aspx.

Hoefer, George. "Tales of Two Jazzmen: One True, Other False." *Down Beat*, April 18, 1952, 7.

Hogan, Ed. "Eddie Levert." AllMusic. www.allmusic.com/artist/eddie-levert-p98018/biography.

Huey, Steve. "Martha Reeves." AllMusic. www.allmusic.com/artist/martha-reeves-p117621/biography.

Hughes, Charles L. Hughes. "Wilson Pickett." Encyclopedia of Alabama. December 3, 2007. www.encyclopediaofalabama.org/face/Article. jsp?id=h-1394.

"Hugh Martin." Songwriters Hall of Fame—Virtual Museum Home. songwritershalloffame.org/index.php/exhibits/bio/C223.

"In Memoriam: Wilson Pickett, 1941–2005." *Popular Music & Society*, July 2006, 387–88.

Integrity Music. www.integritymusic.com.

Jackson, Nancy. "Still Like That Old Time Rock and Roll." Preservation Nation. September 15, 2006. www.preservationnation.org/magazine/story-of-the-week/2006/still-like-that-old-time-rock.html.

"James Joiner." Alabama Music Hall of Fame. www.alamhof.org/jamesjoiner.html.

Jessen, Wade. "Vern Gosdin, 74." *Billboard*, May 9, 2009, 8.

"Jim Cavender." AllAboutJazz.com. December 30, 2008. www.allaboutjazz. com/php/musician.php?id=17713.

"Jim Mahaffey." FJH Music Company Inc. www.fjhmusic.com/composer/jmahaffey.htm.

"Jim Mahaffey." Jim Mahaffey: Composer, Arranger, Educator. jimmahaffey. com/jm-biography1.html.

"Jim Nabors Official Website—History." Jim Nabors Official Website. www.jimnabors.com/history.html.

Jones, Quincy. "Dinah." *Q: The Autobiography of Quincy Jones*. New York: Doubleday, 2001.

Jones, Tina Naremore. "Adele 'Vera' Hall Ward." Encyclopedia of Alabama. January 7, 2008. www.encyclopediaofalabama.org/face/Article.jsp?id=h-1419.

———. "Ruby Pickens Tartt." Encyclopedia of Alabama. March 21, 2007. www.encyclopediaofalabama.org/face/Article.jsp?id=h-1132.

"J.R. Baxter." Southern Gospel Music Association. www.sgma.org/inductee_bios/jr_baxter.htm.

Jung, Fred. "A Fireside Chat with Billy Bang." AllAboutJazz.com. November 14, 2003. www.allaboutjazz.com/php/article.php?id=711.

Karlovits, Bob. "Violinist Says Iraq Experience Echoes Vietnam." *Pittsburgh Tribune-Review*, November 6, 2008.

Krikorian, Dave. "Williams, Cootie (Charles Melvin)." Jazz.com. www.jazz.com/encyclopedia/williams-cootie-charles-melvin.

Landt, Skip, and Fran Landt. "Various: Bullfrog Jumped: Children's Folksongs from the Byron Arnold Collection. (Sound recording review)." *Sing Out!* Sing Out Corporation. 2007. *HighBeam Research*. September 7, 2010.

Lange, Jeffrey J. "Hank Williams Sr." Encyclopedia of Alabama. March 19, 2007. encyclopediaofalabama.org/face/Article.jsp?id=h-1124.

"Lee Stripling: Documentary." Lee Stripling: Home. www.leestripling.com/documentary.aspx.

Lilly, John F. "The Delmore Brothers—A History." Native Ground Books & Music. nativeground.com/articles/99-the-delmore-brothers-by-john-lilly.html.

Loftus, Johnny. "Bo Bice." AOL Music. music.aol.com/artist/bo-bice/biography.

Longino, Miriam. "Three Questions for Toni Tennille." *Atlanta Journal-Constitution*, Apr 13, 1999, B1.

"Lucky Millinder." AllAboutJazz.com. June 25, 2007. www.allaboutjazz.com/php/musician.php?id=9411.

"The Malaco Story." Malaco. www.malaco.com/story.php.

Mather, Shaun. "Mack Vickery." The Official Rockabilly Hall of Fame. December 2002. www.rockabillyhall.com/MackVickery1.html.

Matthews, Burgin. "Mack Vickery Live at the Alabama Women's Prison at Lady Muleskinner Press." Lady Muleskinner Press. November 17, 2008. ladymuleskinnerpress.com/2008/11/mack-vickery-live-at-the-alabama-womens-prison.

Maurer, David. "Goin' to the Chapel for Jazz." America's Intelligence Wire. April 10, 2009. General OneFile. find.galegroup.com/gps/infomark.do?&contentSet =IAC-Documents&type=retrieve&tabID=T004&prodId=IPS&docId=A197630159&source=gale&srcprod=ITOF &userGroupName=avlr&version=1.0.

Mcneil, W.K. *Encyclopedia of American Gospel Music.* 1st ed. New York: Routledge, 2005.

Morrow, John. "The Louvin Brothers." eNotes. www.enotes.com/contemporary-musicians/louvin-brothers-biography.

Mueller, Michael E. "Take 6." eNotes. www.enotes.com/contemporary-musicians/take-6-biography.

"Nat King Cole." *Gale—Home.* www.gale.cengage.com/free_resources/bhm/bio/cole_n.htm.

"Nat King Cole." Starpulse.com. www.starpulse.com/Music/Cole,_Nat_King/Biography.

Noller, Jeremy. "Cootie Williams." AllAboutJazz.com. July 9, 2008. www.allaboutjazz.com/php/musician.php?id=11382.

———. "Eric Essix." AllAboutJazz.com. December 29, 2006. www.allaboutjazz.com/php/musician.php?id=14406.

———. "Ray Reach." AllAboutJazz.com. May 1, 2004. www.allaboutjazz.com/php/musician.php?id=1874.

"Odetta." eNotes. www.enotes.com/contemporary-musicians/odetta-biography.

Oliver, Phillip. "W.C. Handy." University of North Alabama. www.una.edu/library/about/collections/handy/biography.html.

"Opry's Ernie Ashworth Dies." Country Standard Time News Magazine. March 2, 2009. www.countrystandardtime.com/news/newsitem.asp?xid=2643.

"'Pap' Baxter Singing School Revives Shape-Note Tradition." *Chattanooga Times Free Press*, September 10, 2010. www.timesfreepress.com/news/2010/sep/10/pap-baxter-singing-school-revives-shape-note-tradi.

"Pinetop Smith." The Blues Trail. www.thebluestrail.com/artists/mus_cs.htm.

"Profile: Billy Bang and the Making of His Recent Album, 'Vietnam: The Aftermath,' Based on His Experiences in Vietnam." *Weekend Edition Saturday*, January 3, 2004. find.galegroup.com/gps/infomark.do?&contentSet=IAC-Documents&type=retrieve&tabID=T005&prodId=IPS&docId=A161984627&source=gale&srcprod=ITOF&userGroupName=avlr&version=1.0.

"Rich Amerson." 50 Miles of Elbow Room. www.50milesofelbowroom.com/artists/amerson.html.

Robb, Frances O. "Denson Brothers." Encyclopedia of Alabama. February 23, 2007. encyclopediaofalabama.org/face/Article.jsp?id=h-1041.

Roberts, Charles Kenneth. "Blind Boys of Alabama." Encyclopedia of Alabama. May 14, 2009. www.encyclopediaofalabama.org/face/Article.jsp?id=h-2149.

Robertson, David. *W.C. Handy: The Life and Times of the Man Who Made the Blues*. New York: Alfred A. Knopf, 2009.

"Rufus 'Tee-Tot' Payne." The Cosmic American. August 9, 2006. www.thecosmicamerican.com/2006/08/rufus-tee-tot-payne.html.

Ryan, James Emmett. "Emmylou Harris." Encyclopedia of Alabama. December 3, 2007. www.encyclopediaofalabama.org/face/Article.jsp?id=h-1395.

"Sam Phillips' Sun Records." The History of Rock and Roll. www.history-of-rock.com/sam_phillips_sun_records.htm.

"Sanford Kulkin." Spoke.com. www.spoke.com/info/pF3Vvcv/SanfordKulkin.

"The Secret Sisters." The Secret Sisters. www.secretsistersband.com/about.html.

Self, Greg, "Baxter, Jesse Randall [J.R.]." Handbook of Texas Online. www.tshaonline.org/handbook/online/articles/fbaep.

Short, Dale. "UAB's Jazz Man: Cleveland Eaton." *UAB Magazine* 17, no. 4 (Fall 1997). main.uab.edu/show.asp?durki=49269.

Solomon, Olivia, and Jack Solomon. *Honey in the Rock: The Ruby Pickens Tartt Collection of Religious Folk Songs from Sumter County, Alabama*. Macon, GA: Mercer, 2002.

"Sonny James." Sonny James: The Official Site of the Southern Gentleman. www.sonnyjames.com.

Stark, Karl. "Space Is the Place: The Lives and Times of Sun Ra, by John F. Szwed; Pantheon." *Philadelphia Inquirer*, September 27, 1997.

Stone, Peter. "Dock Reed." Association for Cultural Equity. www.culturalequity.org/alanlomax/ce_alanlomax_profile_doc_reed.php.

———. "Vera Ward Hall." Association for Cultural Equity. www.culturalequity.org/alanlomax/ce_alanlomax_profile_hall.php.

"The Stripling Brothers." Welcome to Alabama Arts. www.arts.state.al.us/actc/compilation/wolves.html.

Summers, Kim. "Toni Tennille." Billboard.com. www.billboard.com/artist/toni-tennille/3631#/artist/toni-tennille/bio/3631.

"Susanna Phillips." IMGArtists.com. August 24, 2010. www.imgartists.com/?page=artist&id=710&c=2.

"The Swingle Singers." The Swingle Singers. www.swinglesingers.com/media/official-biographies/group-long-version.html.

"Taylor Hicks." Biography.com. www.biography.com/articles/Taylor-Hicks-589222.

"The Temptations." Lyrics. www.sing365.com/music/lyric.nsf/The-Temptations-Biography/3F34FB517A57747648256D2F002C2A95.

"Tommy Shaw." AOL Music. music.aol.com/artist/tommy-shaw/biography.

"Tommy Stewart." AllAboutJazz.com. December 25, 2006. www.allaboutjazz.com/php/musician.php?id=14395.

"Trail of the Hellhound: W.C. Handy." U.S. National Park Service. www.nps.gov/history/delta/Blues/people/wc_handy.htm.

Valencia, David. "Mitchell & Ruff: An American Profile in Jazz." *Library Journal* 125, no. 16 (2000): 104.

"The Vandellas." The History of Rock and Roll. www.history-of-rock.com/vandellas.htm.

Walker, Bruce. " Green, Urbie." eNotes. www.enotes.com/contemporary-musicians/green-urbie-biography.

Walsh, Mike. "Sun Ra: Stranger from the Outer Space." missionCREEP. missioncreep.com/mw/sunra.html.

Ward, Brian. "Civil Rights and Rock and Roll: Revisiting the Nat King Cole Attack of 1956." *OAH Magazine of History* 24, no. 2 (April 2010): 21.

"Ward Swingle." Singers.com. www.singers.com/arrangers/wardswingle.html.

"Watters Brothers." AllAboutJazz.com. April 6, 2008. www.allaboutjazz.com/php/musician.php?id=16575.

Weaver, Neal. "Howlin' Blues & Dirty Dogs: The Life of Big Mama Thornton." *Back Stage, National ed.*, February 5, 2009, 18. General OneFile. find.galegroup. com/gps/infomark.do?&contentSet=IAC-Documents&type=retrieve&tabID=T003&prodId=IPS&docId=A1939589 75&source=gale&srcprod=ITOF&userGroupName=avlr&version=1.0.

Weiner, Tim. "Odetta, Voice of Civil Rights Movement, Dies at 77." *New York Times*, December 3, 2008. www.nytimes.com/2008/12/03/arts/music/03odetta.html.

White, Chris. "Dr. Hook & the Medicine Show." Lyrics. www.sing365.com/music/lyric.nsf/Dr-Hook-the-Medicine-Show-Biography/3E18B81CF8 51140D48256CAA000FD63E.

Whitsett, Tim, III. "Eddie Floyd." Eddie Floyd. www.eddiefloyd.com.

"Wiley Walker." .music (dotMusic). www.music.us/biography/artist/30076/wiley_walker.html.

"William L. Dawson." Tuskegee University. www.tuskegee.edu/Global/ story.asp?S=1199940.

"William Levi Dawson, African American Composer & Choral Director." AfriClassical. chevalierdesaintgeorges.homestead.com/dawson.html.

Willman, Chris. "The Civil Wars." The Civil Wars. thecivilwars.com.

Wilson, Claire M. "Jim Nabors." Encyclopedia of Alabama. September 1, 2009. www.encyclopediaofalabama.org/face/Article.jsp?id=h-2433.

Wilson, MacKenzie. "Azure Ray." Starpulse.com. www.starpulse.com/ Music/Azure_Ray/Biography.

Wise, Jacob. "Sammy Lowe." AllAboutJazz.com. July 17, 2005. www. allaboutjazz.com/php/musician.php?id=2679.

Yanow, Scott. "Joe Guy." AOL Music. music.aol.com/artist/joe-guy/ biography.

About the Author

C.S. Fuqua is a full-time freelance writer whose published books include *Trust Walk* (collected short fiction), *Big Daddy's Gadgets*, *The Swing: Poems of Fatherhood*, *Divorced Dads* and *Notes to My Becca*, among others. His work has appeared widely in publications as diverse as the *Christian Science Monitor*, *Naval History*, *Main Street Rag* and *Year's Best Horror Stories*. His interest in music history is rooted in his hobbies as a musician and craftsman of Native American flutes. Please visit his website at www.fluteflights.com/CSFUQUA.

Visit us at
www.historypress.net

www.ingramcontent.com/pod-product-compliance
Lightning Source LLC
Chambersburg PA
CBHW070838100426
42813CB00003B/666